YOU CAN
write a song

by Amy Appleby

W9-BSA-990

Order No. AM 932316
US International Standard Book Number: 0.8256.1513.5
UK International Standard Book Number: 0.7119.5211.6

Exclusive Distributors:
Music Sales Corporation
257 Park Avenue South, New York, NY 10010 USA
Music Sales Limited
8/9 Frith Street, London W1V 5TZ England
Music Sales Pty. Limited
120 Rothschild Street, Rosebery, Sydney, NSW 2018, Australia

Printed and bound in the United States of America by
Vicks Lithograph and Printing

Amsco Publications
New York • London • Paris • Sydney

Compact Disc Track Listing

Table of Contents

Introduction

This complete music instruction studio will develop and strengthen your ability to write songs in a variety of popular styles. Whether you are writing for pleasure or profit, you'll find that this professional approach brings great results during every stage of your writing process.

This self-study program focuses on songwriting workshop sessions, which are specially designed to make your creative time productive and fun. These sessions give you the chance to write songs in different styles, including rock, pop, blues, and country music. Songwriters of all levels benefit from this approach, which allows you to develop your own personal writing style—and expand your creative experience. Along the way, you'll get professional tips and guidelines that will bring out the best in every aspect of your original song material. These useful ideas and concepts will continue to serve as a handy reference and source of inspiration throughout your songwriting career.

For easy recognition, hit songs referenced in this book are identified with the artists who made them famous rather than the lyricist or songwriter. If you are interested in learning more about specific songwriters—and their other work—consult one of the many excellent popular music histories.

Choosing a Theme

Your goal as a songwriter is to touch the listener with a subject of importance to his or her life. The theme you choose for a song will naturally be reflected in its title, lyrics, melody, and harmony. If all the components of your song work together to support a strong and commercially viable theme—you've got a hit on your hands.

Professional songwriters will tell you that there are only a handful of basic themes used in popular music. The trick is to develop one of these time-honored subjects in a fresh and up-to-date way. If you are writing songs for use in school, church, or community plays or concerts—you have much more freedom when it comes to choosing a song subject. If you plan to target your songs for children, or another specialty audience, your themes will naturally be quite different from typical popular themes. However, if you want to write mainstream pop/rock songs, you'll want to stick to the themes outlined below.

Although a song should focus on a single central theme, there are times when you will want to incorporate related themes (or sub-themes) in the lyric. This can add psychological truth to your main theme—and make it understandable and appealing. For instance, Elton John's "Rocket Man" focuses on a detailed portrait of a space traveller in tomorrow's world. Yet, the song relies on several general themes for its meaning: loneliness, love, family, and day-to-day survival.

Here's a rundown of the theme categories used in commercially successful songs. As you might expect, many of these center on love—the favorite theme of songwriters since the beginning of written history.

Looking for Love. Lonely hearts and would-be lovers are portrayed in many a pop song. A few examples are: "Lookin' for Love," "I Ain't Got Nobody," "I Want to Know What Love Is," and "Alone."

Proposing Love. Some song lyrics center on an invitation to love, like "I Want to Hold Your Hand," "Don't You Want Me," "Do Ya Think I'm Sexy," "Get Outta My Dreams, Get Into My Car," and "Baby, Come to Me."

Making Love. Each passing year brings more and more explicit celebrations of physical love on the hit charts. Although most radio stations and record companies still draw the line at rough language, many songs with openly sexual themes have climbed high on the charts. These include: "Feel Like Makin' Love," "Love to Love You Baby," "It's the Right Time of the Night," "Do That to Me One More Time," "Like a Virgin," and "I Want Your Sex."

Celebrating Love. Lovers in love are the theme of countless pop songs, including "You Are the Sunshine of My Life," "Together Forever," "Groovy Kind of Love," "Up Where We Belong," and "Nothing's Gonna Stop Us Now."

Unrequited Love. Several major hits deal with one-sided love—whether it's from the point of view of the pursuer or the pursued. Here's just a few: "Don't Be Cruel," "You Give Love a Bad Name," "Every Breath You Take," and "I'm Gonna Knock on Your Door."

Broken Love. This is a powerful song theme that works best in slow songs like "Where Do Broken Hearts Go," "She's Out of My Life," and "The Way We Were."

Personal Portraits. Many songs paint a portrait of an interesting character, such as "Piano Man," "Who's That Girl," "Maniac," "Desperado," and "Private Dancer." A few portrait songs present sketches of two or more characters, such as "Eleanor Rigby" and "I'm Not Lisa." Others pay tribute to actual persons such as "Vincent" (a portrait of Vincent Van Gogh), "Candle in the Wind" (on the life of Marilyn Monroe), and "Abraham, Martin, and John" (in memory of Abraham Lincoln, Martin Luther King, and John and Bobby Kennedy). Songs with personal portraits always draw on other universal themes for their meaning. For instance, "Desperado" is really about the difficulty of self-realization—and "Eleanor Rigby" illustrates societal loneliness and separation.

Places and Objects. Some songs depict a place, real or fictional, like "MacArthur Park" or "Somewhere Over the Rainbow." Others describe a meaningful object like "The Rose" or "Purple Rain." Portraits of places or objects are usually linked with broader themes, such as love or self-realization.

Events. Some popular songs recount a meaningful story or pay tribute to a particular event, either real or fictional. These include: "The Night They Drove Old Dixie Down," "New York Mining Disaster 1941," "American Pie," and "Night Chicago Died." Although these songs often feature characters, the main thrust is the event itself and its broad-reaching effects. Other songs deal with time in a more general sense, such as "Forever" or "When Doves Cry."

Friendship. A few major hits deal with friendship rather than romantic love. These include: "With a Little Help From My Friends," "You've Got a Friend," "That's What Friends Are For," and "Lean on Me."

Family. Relationships between family members are portrayed in selected pop hits, such as "Father and Son," "Cat's in the Cradle," "Daniel," "My Mother's Eyes," and "Papa Was a Rolling Stone."

Self-Realization. Certain pop songs deal with an individual's self-realization or personal view of life. Although this is a relatively small category, some memorable hits include: "Man in the Mirror," "At Seventeen," "Tapestry," "I Am a Rock," and "From Both Sides Now." Take care when developing this theme that you don't wax melodramatic—or present problems and pains that others can not relate to easily.

Dance. A relatively large number of pop hits focus on the theme of dancing or dancers. Songs with this theme are generally intended as uptempo dance numbers. Here are just a few: "Dance With Me," "Dancing Queen," "Flashdance," and "Neutron Dance." Certain dance songs introduce or capitalize on particular dance crazes. These include "Twist and Shout," "The Hustle," "Disco Lady," and "Vogue." Be careful when planning a song with this type of dance theme: it's unlikely that a developing songwriter would be able to introduce a new dance without industry support. If you're planning to write a song that capitalizes on an existing dance craze, you may find the fad is over by the time your demo gets heard. You're better off writing about dancing in general (just be sure that your music reflects the latest in dance club grooves—and that your lyric is simple, exciting, and memorable).

Music. Many songs celebrate music itself. These may be either uptempo songs or ballads, such as: "I Love Music," "I Love Rock 'n Roll," "It's Still Rock and Roll to Me," "Rock Me Amadeus," and "There'll Be Sad Songs (To Make You Cry)." A few hits have explored the subject of music from the songwriter's point of view ("I Write the Songs" and "Your Song"), but this is an inadvisable theme for the developing songwriter.

Novelty. From time to time, a song with a novel or humorous theme makes it on the charts, such as: "The Monster Mash," "Junk Food Junkie," and "Ghostbusters." In industry terms, a novelty song features humorous characters and incorporates patter, nonsense words, or special effects, as in "My Ding-a-Ling," "Disco Duck," "Chipmunk Song" or "Jingle Bells" (by the Barking Dogs). However, certain mainstream pop numbers also feature novel subjects, such as "Walk Like an Egyptian," "She Bop," and "Spiders and Snakes." Although this is not a large category in today's music, a well-crafted novelty song may be just the thing to turn heads in a producer's office. Keep in mind, however, the success of a novelty song is often dependent on the songwriter's sophisticated sense of timing—and a record company's strong promotional effort.

Fantasy. Fantasies and dreams have served as the theme for a few prominent hits, including: "Lucy in the Sky With Diamonds," "Ghost Riders in the Sky," "La Isla Bonita," and "One Night in Bangkok." Like novelty songs, these should be very neatly crafted—yet give the impression of subconscious thinking and free association. This poses a great challenge for the developing lyricist.

Work, Money, and Survival. Some pop songs focus on the theme of survival in the work-a-day world. These include: "9 to 5," "Nightshift," "Money," "She Works Hard for the Money," "Living for the City," "Morning Train (9 to 5)," and "Car Wash."

Philosophical/Moral. Racial harmony, sexual equality, crime, drugs, and other social issues have served as the theme for selected commercial hits, such as: "Ebony and Ivory," "Papa Don't Preach," "Beat It," and "Don't Worry Be Happy." The only songs in this category that gain wide acceptance are those which do not involve the listener in a moral lecture. Many developing songwriters make the mistake of trying to improve society rather than entertaining them. Your first goal is to write good songs. If your work makes people feel better about themselves or draws their attention to society's problems, that's an added plus. If you do choose a moral theme for one of your songs, please be sure you believe in your message— and that it is stated clearly. Also be aware of its possible repercussions. Hundreds, if not thousands, of babies were born to unemployed and homeless teenage mothers as a result of Madonna's song "Papa Don't Preach." Social workers and adoption counselors throughout the country will attest to the many sad results of this song's popularity.

Political/Patriotic. A few successful hits focus on political or patriotic themes, such as "Africa," "We Are the World," "Bangladesh," "Allentown," and "Ohio." Generally speaking, record companies veer away from material that is politically controversial—so stick to subjects of universal importance like world peace, ecology, or equal rights. Even these broad topics must be handled with care if you want to create commercially successful songs. Most listeners prefer to learn about these subjects from the news-paper and television news—and turn to music to take their mind off world affairs. A broad, optimistic theme like "We Are the World" is perhaps the safest choice in this category.

The Hit Title

Many songwriters begin with nothing more than a title that they believe in—and build the rest of the song around it. Although songs often receive a title in later stages of the songwriting process—many other successful hits are fashioned from a single meaningful phrase.

A song title should represent the subject matter or theme of your song. Some titles sum up the song's theme in a direct and straightforward manner, as in "I Wanna Dance With Somebody (Who Loves Me)" or "Saving All My Love for You." Others titles are explained during the course of the song. For instance, the song lyric of "Ebony and Ivory" gradually reveals the symbolism of the title: As the black and white keys of the piano work together to create musical harmony, so should love and cooperation exist between the races. This wonderful title uses symbolism to handle the delicate and important issue of race relations. This song would certainly never have made it with a straightforward title like "Hey, Black and White People Should Cooperate." In this section, you'll learn many professional techniques for creating effective and memorable titles for your own songs. Remember, the title of your song is the first thing that publishers learn about your work—so it really pays to get their attention right from the start.

Title Format

There are hundreds of different kinds of song titles, but only three basic title formats: label, statement, and question. When you are choosing a title for a song, create a working title in each of these formats—then pick the one that serves your theme best.

Label. Many songs use a simple label as a title. This is a great way to capture the essence of a song in a nutshell. A label title is a good choice for songs that portray a person, place, quality, or thing in a straightforward and meaningful way. If your song theme can be captured in a simple and interesting label title, don't hesitate to use it. This kind of title has worked in thousands of song hits, such as "Car Wash," "Dreams," "Magic," "The Flame," and "Man in the Mirror."

Statement. Many titles consist of a clear statement that sums up the theme of the song. In fact, it's often a good idea to think of a topic statement for your song as a working title to keep you on track during the creative process. You can always shorten or change the title later when the song is more fully formed. Sometimes title statements are pure and simple, as in "I Just Can't Stop Loving You" or "You Give Love a Bad Name." Other statements need to be explained in the song lyric, such as "That's What Friends Are For" or "Here I Go Again." Some titles work best as partial statements, as in "Lost in Emotion," "Anything for You," "At This Moment," "When I Think of You," or "The Next Time I Fall." Others title statements are completed in parenthetical phrases, as in "(I Just) Died in Your Arms" and "I Wanna Dance With Somebody (Who Loves Me)." In most cases, you should choose the shortest possible statement phrase that summarizes your theme—and explain the rest in the song lyric.

Titles that offer a statement in the form of a **command** (like "Jump" or "Shout") actively involve the listener in the song's action. These are particularly appropriate when you want to get people dancing or tapping their toes. Some titles address the listener with a gentler command, such as "Lean on Me," "Don't Worry Be Happy," or "Take It Easy." Other commands bring the song's characters to life, as in "Get Outta My Dreams, Get Into My Car," "Papa Don't Preach," or "Don't Lose My Number." Like the question title, the command establishes the singer as a purposeful narrator/character in the song with a strong goal or need.

Question. The *interrogative mood* of a question is a good way to capture the listener's attention. The song itself answers the question (or explores the possibilities for an answer), as in "Who Will You Run To Tomorrow" or "How Will I Know." (Notice that modern convention requires no question mark in these titles.) Using a question as your title sets the stage for a first-person narrative—that is, the singer becomes a narrator/character of the song in search of an answer. A *rhetorical question* implies its own answer, as in "What's Love Got to Do With It" (not much), "Who Do You Think You're Foolin'" (not me), and "Is a Blue Bird Blue" (without a doubt). This is a clever way to involve your listener in answering the question as you pose it.

Figures of Speech

Here's a rundown of some of the techniques professional songwriters use to make their titles memorable and meaningful. These same *figures of speech* are also very useful when it comes to writing the song's lyrics. Don't feel obligated to use any of these constructions if you already have a strong, unadorned label or statement title. These figures only work when they crystallize the meaning of your theme neatly and naturally—but never when they are forced into place.

Symbolism. Some titles offer a symbol of their theme, as in "Broken Wings," "Red Red Wine," or "The Long and Winding Road." It's easy to make assumptions about the theme of each of these songs from the title alone, for they are psychologically meaningful across the globe. Wings symbolize freedom, red wine connotes passion, and a long road is the path of life. Even Prince's very original symbol "Purple Rain" stirs our ancestral identification of rain with sorrow—and the color purple with importance and drama. The symbol in a song title is often explained directly in the lyric using *metaphor* or *simile* (defined below). Nevertheless, stick to symbols that everyone understands—or plan to devote the entire lyric to explaining a novel or little known symbol (as in "Tie a Yellow Ribbon Round the Ole Oak Tree").

Metaphor. Symbolism may be outlined literally in metaphor, which identifies the symbol directly with the thing represented (usually using the words "are" or "is"). Some strong title metaphors include "Love Is a Rose," "We Are the World," "I Am a Rock," "You Are the Sunshine of My Life," and "Heaven Is a Place on Earth."

Simile. In some song titles, symbolism is outlined in simile, which likens by similarity (usually with the words "like" or "as"). Some memorable similes include: "Like a Virgin," "Fly Like an Eagle," and "Like a Prayer."

Personification. Some songs give human attributes to things and concepts, as in "Good Morning Heartache," "Bridge Over Troubled Water," and "You Give Love a Bad Name." Some titles objectify or depersonalize human attributes, as in "Dial My Heart" or "I Am a Rock."

Overstatement. Also called *hyperbole,* overstatement is used in many a song title. This figure of speech naturally gives a feeling of scope and drama to a title, as in "End of the World," "Cry Me a River," "Everybody Wants to Rule the World," "50 Ways to Leave Your Lover," "I Only Have Eyes for You," and "Goin' out of My Head." Overstatement is particularly effective in song titles that focus on love (or the lack of it).

Understatement. Although less common than overstatement, understatement (also called *litotes*) can be effective in a title. This figure treats typically important issues in an off-handed and restrained manner, as in "Girls Just Want to Have Fun," "Give Peace a Chance," or "I Haven't Got Time for the Pain."

Allusion. Many hit titles are immediately recognizable and memorable because they allude to familiar phrases. These include "Knock on Wood," "Head to Toe," "When the Going Gets Tough, the Tough Get Going," "Time After Time," and "9 to 5." Some very effective song titles put an unexpected twist on a familiar phrase, as in "Hurts So Good," "Total Eclipse of the Heart," "Shadow Dancing" "(Love Is) Thicker Than Water," or "Love You Inside Out." Using a familiar phrase in a title is an excellent way to get welcome recognition from your listeners. A select few titles allude to well-known works of literature, like "Jacob's Ladder," "Richard Cory," "Kyrie," "White Rabbit," and "Goodbye Yellow Brick Road." Others allude to television and movies ("Bette Davis Eyes") or even serve as their theme songs ("Ghostbusters" and "Theme From Mahogany"). Some song titles mention other songs, or even reuse titles, as in "Dancing in the Dark," "Small World," and "Dancing on the Ceiling."

Pun. A well-chosen pun can lend a clever double meaning to your title, as in "Private Eyes" or "Wishing Well." Often a punning title gives a humorous effect, as in "I'll Tennessee You in My Dreams" or "If I Said You Have a Beautiful Body Would You Hold It Against Me." Don't try to force a clever pun into a title that doesn't want one. You'll know it right away if the perfect one comes along.

A title should not only reflect the meaning of your song lyric, it should also sound good. As discussed in the next section, you'll probably repeat the title as a key phrase (or *hook*) in the song lyric—so it's important that your title is catchy and natural-sounding when spoken or sung. Here are some figures of speech that songwriters use achieve this effect. You'll also find these constructions very useful when writing the song's lyrics. Again, don't feel obligated to use these constructions if you already have a strong label or statement title. Titles with these figures only work if they also reflect the overall meaning of your song. In other words, the catchy sound they create is just the icing on the cake.

Alliteration. The repetition of consonants is very effective in a song title—and has been used in thousands of songs, including ''Father Figure,'' ''Man in the Mirror,'' and ''My Boyfriend's Back.''

Assonance. Repeated vowel sounds can really make a title catchy, as in ''Ruby Tuesday'' or ''Coward of the County.''

Rhyme. Naturally, a title that rhymes is easy to remember and fun to sing. Think of the rhyming sounds in ''Together Forever,'' ''Kokomo,'' ''Eye of the Tiger'' and ''You Light Up My Life.''

Repetition. Repetition of words can add power and excitement to a song title, as in ''Say Say Say,'' ''Say You Say Me,'' ''Red Red Wine,'' ''Wild, Wild West,'' and ''Too Much, Too Little, Too Late.''

Colloquialisms. Slang and conversational language can be memorable in titles, such as ''Crazy for You,'' ''I Can't Go for That (No Can Do),'' and ''Stuck With You.''

You'll probably explore the possibilities for title and lyric at the same time during the songwriting process. Refer back to this section for title ideas during your writing sessions. Take the time to analyze the titles of the songs you hear—and identify what makes them effective and memorable.

The Hook

As a rule, the title of a song occurs in a key melody phrase of the song called the *hook*. The hook is often repeated one or more times during the song, particularly during the chorus when the excitement is at its peak. The agreement of lyric and music in your song hook is a key factor in the overall success of a given song. Many songwriters start with a hook they like, and then build the rest of the song around it.

In many cases, the title should suggest the best position for the hook in your song. Ending statements, like ''That's What Friends Are For'' or ''It's Still Rock and Roll to Me'' work best at the end of a song section. Beginnings of phrases, like ''Dear Prudence,'' ''Another Saturday Night,'' or ''Oh Very Young'' suggest an early placement in the song (even the first line). Determine the appropriate placement of your song hook in the lyric, then build the rest of the lyric to this logical conclusion.

Remember, many hooks provide a variation of the title—usually an extension. The song ''Can't Help Falling in Love'' (which was a hit for both Elvis Presley and Corey Hart) features a slightly longer hook: ''I can't help falling in love with you.'' Dolly Parton's ''9 to 5'' is ''Workin' 9 to 5'' in the hook. ''Up Where We Belong'' has the hook, ''Love lifts us up where we belong.'' Sometimes the title is not featured as the hook line, as in ''Eleanor Rigby,'' which uses ''All the lonely people'' as the chorus hook. Although a song should technically pivot on one hook line, some songs use auxiliary phrases with the hook. For instance, The Police song ''Every Breath You Take'' features another important hook-like line in the chorus ''I'll be watching you.'' The hook in ''I Just Called to Say I Love You'' occurs regularly with ''And I mean it from the bottom of my heart.''

The melody and rhythm of a song hook should complement the natural rhythm of the words. Try saying the hook you have in mind aloud several times, and make note of its spoken rhythm. Use this as a basis for the rhythm of your melody line. The perfect hook features accented or sustained notes on stressed sylla-bles, and unaccented or short notes on unstressed syllables. Stressed notes usually fall on the beat, as in these titles.

```
| ´   ˘ ˘  | ´ ˘ ´ |
| Born in the | U. S. A. |
˘ | ´ ˘ ´   ´ ˘   |
I | am the Entertainer |
| ´ ˘  ´   ˘ ´ ˘˘  ´ ˘ ´  | ´    |
| I'm just burnin' doin'  the Neutron | Dance |
```

As a general rule, important vowel sounds occur on the accented and sustained notes of the hook. Analyze the hook lines of some of your favorite songs to see this principle in action. You should also consider the natural spoken pitch of your hook line when spoken. Say the hook lyric aloud, and take note of the pitch of your voice. Determine where it moves from high to low (as in "Beat It" or "We Are the World")—or, from low to high (as in "Let's Hear It for the Boy" or "If I Can't Have You").

Meaning can also influence pitch. Questions can cause the hook melody to move upward, as in "Where Is the Love" or "Are You Lonesome Tonight." Commands and statements often feature a descending mel-ody line, as in "Lean on Me" or "Saving All My Love for You." Some hook melodies use note repetition to drive home the point, as in "You Are So Beautiful," "I Think I Love You." A hook melody may move symbolically from low to high to illustrate a positive or hopeful song theme, as in "Morning Has Broken" or "If I Loved You." A more serious or emphatic theme may lead the hook melody downward, as in "Maniac" or "What's Love Got to Do With It."

Take the time to explore the possibilities for natural and meaningful patterns of rhythm and pitch when you write your own hooks. Try out different versions of a hook with melody variations. It really pays off when you find just the right combination of sound and sense. Remember, the hook line is the heart of your song—and the focus of interest for your listeners.

Melody Form

Some hit songs begin as a catchy melody—and the lyric is added later. Many songwriters find success with this approach, especially when working with a lyricist. Unlike the melody of a symphony or instrumental solo, a song melody is meant to be sung. Although many song melodies sound great as instrumentals, very few popular hits are created for this setting (and true instrumental hits like "Music Box Dancer" or "Chariots of Fire" are not technically considered songs). Thus, the experienced song melodist is naturally quite aware of the powers and limitations of language and the human voice. Your understanding of the form and phrasing of a song's melody and words will help you develop and shape your own tunes into excellent song material.

A song melody is made up of individual lines or *melodic phrases* which correspond to lines of the *song lyric*. Just as each line of the lyric expresses a different thought, each phrase of the melody expresses a new "musical idea." Most popular songs follow a melody formula called *question and answer*. This ancient melody form has its roots in the earliest Western music. Songwriters often plan the phrasing pattern of their melody very early in the writing process. This helps determine the overall structure of the song sections—and the structure of the song's lyrics and harmony.

The traditional favorite "Scarborough Fair" features a basic question-and-answer pattern. Each verse of the song is made up of four melodic phrases of equal length. These correspond to four lines of lyric. In each verse, a two-line question is followed by a two-line answer.

Notice that the first two lines move gradually upward in pitch, much like a spoken question. The answer phrase moves downward in pitch, as would a spoken statement. The highest notes of the melody occur at the beginning of the answer—a strong place for the *climax* of the melody. This question-and-answer pattern is repeated in each subsequent verse of "Scarborough Fair." Let's take a look at how the melodic pattern is mirrored in the song's lyric.

Lyric

Your main goal when writing a song lyric is to explain and celebrate the song's overall theme through story and symbolism. As you know, a good lyric also reflects the musical structure of a song—and this correspondence is an essential factor in its success. This important relationship is what distinguishes the song lyric from a poem—the singer from a speaker. In this section, you'll learn how to use lyrical rhythm and rhyme to complement the musical rhythm and structure of song.

Stress

The spoken rhythm of a song's words suggests a natural pattern of stress. Note how the note durations in the melody of Simon and Garfunkel's *Scarborough Fair* match the natural accents of the lyric. The strong first beat of the measure always has a word with a natural accent.

Rhyme Scheme

A song's structure is pointed up by the use of rhyming words at the end of each line. In "Scarborough Fair," alternating lines of the lyric rhyme, as indicated by the letters *A* and *B*.

A

Are you going to Scarborough Fair;

B

Parsley, sage, rosemary, and thyme?

A

Remember me to one who lives there,

B

For she once was a true love of mine.

Notice that the words "Fair" and "there" form a *true* or *perfect rhyme*—while "thyme" and "mine" form a *false* or *imperfect rhyme*. The two words that make up an imperfect rhyme should be similar sounding enough to give the effect of a rhyme. This type of rhyming is common in pop and rock music—and can even help contribute to its natural and free-wheeling sound.

The second verse of "Scarborough Fair" relies entirely on imperfect rhyme. Yet, the rhyming pairs "mine" and "thyme"—and "shirt" and "needlework"—sound close enough to rhyme in this folk setting. ("Needlework" technically forms a *masculine rhyme* because it is the final syllable, "-work," which rhymes with "shirt.")

A

Tell her to make me a cambric shirt,

B

Parsley, sage, rosemary, and thyme;

A

One with no seam or fine needlework,

B

And then she'll be a true love of mine.

Same-Word Rhymes and Repetition

Sometimes the same word is used to form a rhyme, as in the end of lines one and three of "Morning Has

Broken." The lyricist has also made use of repeated words in this verse to enhance the simple truth of its message. Words that are repeated within the verse are shown in italics.

A

Morning has broken, *like the first morning.*

B

Black*bird has* spoken, *like the first bird.*

A

Praise for the singing; *praise for the morning;*

B

Praise for them, springing fresh from the Word!

Internal Rhyme

This song also uses *internal rhyme* to point up the relationship between phrases, as indicated by the letters *C* and *D*.

C

Morning has broken, like the first morning.

C

Blackbird has spoken, like the first bird.

D

Praise for the singing; praise for the morning;

D

Praise for them, springing fresh from the Word!

These two-syllable or *double rhymes* are considered *feminine rhymes,* because of the stress on the first syllable ("**brok**-en" and "**spok**-en").

Multiple Rhyme

Let's explore the further use of multiple rhymes in verse three of "Morning Has Broken." Here double internal rhymes ("sunlight" and "one light"), as well as *triple rhymes* ("elation" and "-creation") provide an intricate internal pattern. Contrastingly, lines one and three provide a same-word rhyme with "morning"—and a simple rhyme lends a sense of finality to lines two and four ("play" and "day").

C   A

Mine is the sunlight, mine is the morning

C   B

Born of the one light Eden saw play.

D   A

Praise with elation, praise every morning,

D   B

God's re-creation of the new day.

The intricately woven rhyme scheme of "Morning Has Broken" is certainly not the norm in pop and rock music. However, this heavy use of rhyme can be hauntingly effective in songs with a simple setting and traditional theme.

As you study this lead sheet of "Morning Has Broken," notice how the rhymes at the ends of lines emphasize the overall question-and-answer pattern of the melody. The internal rhyme scheme and repeated words suggest a regular pattern of sub-phrases. These sub-phrases are called *motifs*—and give the effect of smaller questions and answers within the larger phrases.

To strengthen your ability to identify different types of rhymes, analyze the rhyme scheme and use of word repetition in one or more of these pop/rock hits.

"Love Is a Rose"   "The First Time Ever I Saw Your Face"
"Lovely Rita, Meter Maid"   "The Rose"

Song Forms

Almost every song is made up of individual *song sections*. The pattern of these sections determines the song's overall *form* or *structure*. A strong and appropriate song form is of vital importance to its success as a hit. In fact, your first goal as you develop a new song should be to work to create a simple and strong structure that shows off your music and words to their best advantage. Here's a rundown of the basic song sections you can use to structure a song.

Verse. The verse section of the song usually provides some basic information about the song's setting, mood, and characters. Here, the singer offers important details from a personal point of view; either as a caring narrator or witness—or as a character in the story itself. During the first verse, you should try to involve the listener in the circumstances and musical setting of the song—and to create mounting interest in its outcome. The verse should be designed to lead into the *chorus* or *bridge,* both musically and lyrically.

Each subsequent verse generally features the same music with a different set of words. The second verse advances the story line, circumstances, or emotional development of characters in the song. The final verse brings the story to a conclusion. Sometimes the first verse is repeated as the final verse to bring the story "full circle."

Chorus. The chorus section generally follows the verse and provides a simple and meaningful statement about the song as a whole. The chorus often incorporates the hook of the song in repetition, particularly in the first or last lines. The first chords of the chorus should be the harmonic high point of the song. The chorus is often repeated two or three times during the song with little or no change. Don't be afraid to be plain and simple when writing the chorus—it's the section that the listener is waiting for and the one that you want them to "go out whistling."

Bridge. Also called the *release,* the bridge section provides a departure from the body of the song. This diversion is often just eight bars long—and leads naturally back to the chorus or verse section. The lyric of the bridge often sheds new light on the theme of the song by offering a different point of view, a change of time frame or speaker.

Refrain. A refrain is a simple song section which repeats the last lines of the verse. Although the refrain is common in music of yesteryear, it sounds antiquated today in almost every context.

Instrumental Break. Some songs feature an instrumental section. Although most musical interludes are created as an afterthought by a song's arranger or performers, a few are central to the structure of a song. An instrumental break may occur at the song's beginning, middle, or end. It is usually designed to lead neatly to or from a vocal song section. A break section commonly occurs during the middle of a song, where it provides a brief departure from the body of the song (like a bridge section). Sometimes the break uses the chord pattern of the verse or chorus. Don't feel obligated to use an instrumental break unless it plays an essential role in the structure of your song.

Introduction. Although extended vocal introductions are generally a thing of the past, many of today's songs include a short instrumental introduction. Occasionally, a pop hit uses a vocal intro, as in the spoken section at the beginning of "Ain't No Mountain High Enough," as recorded by Diana Ross—or the hummed intro in Barbra Streisand's "The Way We Were."

Tag. Some songs feature a short section at the end. This tag (or *coda*) may serve to "cap off" the song's ending, as in "Say, Has Anybody Seen My Sweet Gypsy Rose." More often the tag is a repeating fade-out of the hook line itself, as in James Taylor's recording of "You've Got a Friend" or "Take It to the Limit," as recorded by the Eagles.

The Ballad (AAA)

A song with one repeating verse section is known as a *ballad*. Since musicians often refer to the verse as the *A section,* this form is also called *AAA form.* Ballad form is the oldest and simplest song form still used in today's pop music. Centuries ago, the ballad was used in the British Isles not only to entertain, but to relate important stories and news events. Since the musical elements of a ballad remain the same from verse to verse, most songs in this form feature an interesting and varied lyric with several verses. Traditionally, ballads feature a serious theme and a dramatic setting. However, today, the word "ballad" is used to mean any song with a slow tempo—and ballad form is more often referred to as AAA song form. The folk-pop revival of the sixties and seventies brought many traditional ballads to national attention, including "Scarborough Fair," "House of the Rising Sun," and "Sloop John B." Many more contemporary ballads enjoyed fame on the pop charts, including "Color My World" and "Day by Day."

The Verse-Chorus Song (ABAB)

The *verse-chorus song* is the single most popular form used in today's music—especially when it comes to pop and rock. In this song form the verse-chorus pattern is usually repeated several times. In this way, the verse-chorus song is patterned ABAB or ABABAB, as in "Yellow Submarine" or "Lean on Me." Sometimes this form is reversed to produce BABA, as in Simon & Garfunkel's "Cecilia" or Natalie Cole's "This Will Be."

The Verse-Bridge Song (AABA)

The *AABA song form* provides the structure for many jazz standards and show songs of the 1920s, 1930s, and 1940s. This verse-verse-bridge-verse pattern occurs in classics like "Blue Skies" and "Ain't Misbehavin'." During the melody era, the AABA song was often preceded by a substantial introductory verse section. The AABA was considered to be a verse-chorus song, with the AABA pattern forming the chorus section. Today, the introduction no longer occurs with this form—and the AABA pattern is used in its pure form. Some song hits that have used this form include "Memories," from the musical *Cats,* and "The Rose," recorded by Bette Midler.

Chord Chart

A *chord chart* is an arrangement of a song that contains chord symbols only. Take a look at the chord chart for the rock/blues song "Crossroads" that Cream made into a rock and roll hit in 1969. Originally entitled "Crossroad Blues," this song was a favorite of blues master Robert Johnson. A basic chord chart like the one that follows need only show the general outline of the harmony: the name and duration of each chord. Here, four slash marks in each measure represent the four quarter-note beats per measure of $\frac{4}{4}$ time. Many chord charts include more detailed rhythms, as you will see in the next section, "Rhythm and Style."

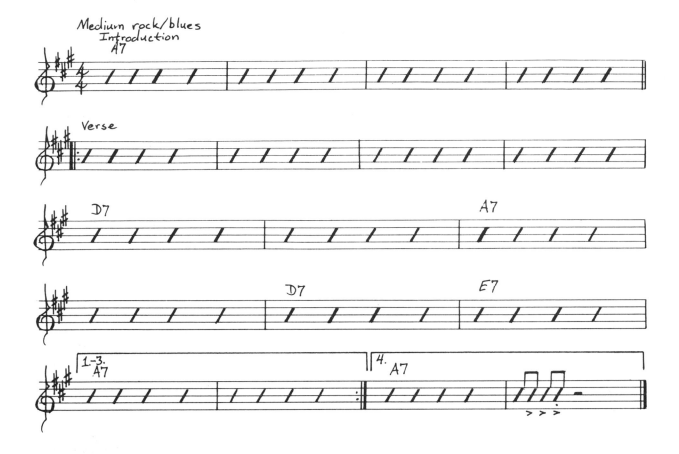

Lead Sheet

A *lead sheet* is a written version of a song which contains the melody, chord symbols, and lyrics. Here's "Crossroads" in lead-sheet form. You should create a lead sheet like this for every song you write. You may want to send your lead sheets to yourself by registered (or certified) mail—and file the unopened envelopes away as proof of their creation dates. This is less expensive than registering your songs with the United States Copyright Office. However, if you choose to register your songs, write to this office to obtain the "PA" form: United States Copyright Office, Library of Congress, Washington, DC 20559. Two lead sheets will be required for each work you wish to have registered.

© 1991 Shirley Trad and Rocky Bluesman (K)

A Title. Place the title at the top and center of the first page of the lead sheet. Use initial capitals on all title words with four letters or more. Always use initial capitals on the first and last word of a title. Don't capitalize articles ("a," "an," and "the"), conjunctions ("and" and "but"), or prepositions ("on," "in," "out," and so on). Capitalize prepositions that are part of a verbal phrase (as in "Roll Out the Barrel"). Avoid subtitles or alternate titles that detract from your phrase of choice.

B Lyricist/Composer. Use initial capitals to credit the lyricist and composer. If the words and music are created by one person, write "Words and music by [name]" in this position.

C Tempo/Feel. Indicate the tempo or feel of your song in this position. Here, a simple instruction like "Medium rock" or "Slow shuffle" is often most useful. Only the first word of the tempo indication should be capitalized.

D Treble Clef. Except in special cases, a lead sheet should be notated in the treble clef. This clef should appear at the beginning of every staff line.

D Key Signature. Be sure to indicate the sharps and flats of the key in a key signature at the beginning of every staff. Choose a key that places the melody in a standard singing range (like soprano, alto, tenor, or bass). Avoid keys with four or more flats or sharps.

E Time Signature. The time signature is written after the key signature at the beginning of the first staff only.

F Riff Figure. Some of the songs you write may feature an important instrumental riff as an integral part of the song structure. A riff may occur at any point during the song. In this example, the riff figure forms the introduction. Don't feel the need to add a riff figure to your lead sheet unless it really needs one. Many riffs should be saved for inclusion in a full arrangement of your song.

G Melody. The complete melody of the song should be clearly notated on the staff. There's no need to write special instructions to the vocalist or notate melody nuances that can be worked out later. Just write the melody in its simplest form, and exclude any decorations that are best added when the song is actually being arranged for recording or performance. Check to make sure that each measure of the melody line is made up of the correct number of beats.

H Lyric. Each syllable of the lyric should correspond with one or more melody notes. Hyphens divide words into syllables. If one syllable lasts for more than one note, the hyphen is centered under the corresponding melody notes. If a word (or the last syllable of a word) is held for two melody notes, it is followed by a horizontal underline. One or two extra verses may be included beneath the first verse (in which case, the verses should be numbered "1," "2," "3," and so on). Some songs feature more than one or two extra verses—and these are best provided at the bottom of the lead sheet in block text (and numbered "2," "3," "4," and so on).

I Chord Symbols. The lead sheet must include chord letter names outlining the harmonic structure of your song. Try not to use unnecessarily complex chords here. Just reduce the harmony to its simple important movements.

J Section Labels. It's helpful to include song section labels—like *Introduction, Verse, Chorus,* and *Tag*—to clarify the overall structure of the song.

K Copyright Notice. Your song is protected by copyright law as soon as it is written. It's a good idea to include a copyright notice at the bottom of your lead sheet with the year and the name of the song's rightful owner.

The Beat

In popular music, the basic underlying rhythm of a song is known variously as the *beat, groove,* or *feel.* It is often the rhythmic feel of a song that most strongly suggests its genre. For example, if you play a blues song with a rock feel, it will most likely sound like a rock song—for the feel gives the listener the most obvious clues.

Popular-music grooves fall into two basic categories: *straight-eighth* and *shuffle* beats. Classical musicians would call these *duple metre* and *triple metre* because in the former the beats in each measure are subdivided into groups of two, while in the latter each beat may be subdivided into a group of three. The most common time signature is $\frac{4}{4}$. Each one of the four quarter-note beats may be subdivided into two eighth-notes or three eighth-notes.

In a straight-eighth $\frac{4}{4}$ groove, there are usually accents on the second and fourth beats. This is known as the *backbeat.* You can also have a straight-eighth feel in $\frac{2}{4}$ time; in this case the backbeat accent occurs on the second beat of every measure. Depending on the type of music, the amount of accent that the backbeat receives may be quite a bit on down to none at all—but it is almost always felt.

In a medium-tempo rock, R&B, or dance song, the basic feel would probably feature a very conspicuous backbeat in response to a driving beat. Bruce Springsteen's "Born in the U.S.A." provides an example of a $\frac{4}{4}$ rock song with a backbeat. A backbeat in $\frac{2}{4}$ is illustrated in M.C. Hammer's "Can't Touch This." In each of these examples the slash marks give you an outline of the basic rhythm, and the powerful backbeat is indicated by accent symbols (⸗).

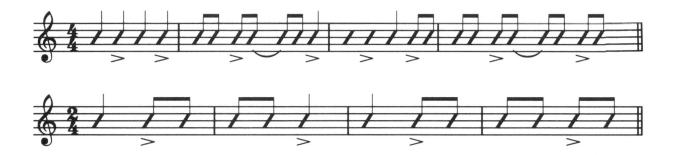

Look at this syncopated $\frac{4}{4}$ groove, which you might hear in a song like Sade's "Smooth Operator." *Syncopation* is caused by notes that anticipate or delay the normal pulse. Note that the last eighth note of both the first and third measures—as well as the tied notes in the middle of the fourth measure—are examples of syncopation. The backbeat (again indicated by the accent symbols) is a lot less prominent here than in the previous examples.

Here's another common $\frac{4}{4}$ rhythmic pattern which features the backbeat on the third beat. This is sometimes called a *half-time feel* because the rhythm sounds like it is going half the speed of the melody. The half-time backbeat feel creates a funky groove in a slow song such as the Pointer Sisters' "Fire."

This backbeat pattern also lends a somewhat loose and laid-back quality to an uptempo number such as the Beatles' "Maxwell's Silver Hammer."

In $\frac{3}{4}$ time, the backbeat—if there is one—may fall either on the second or third beat of the measure. More often, the first beat of the measure is stressed and 2 and 3 remain unaccented.

Here are a few basic shuffle grooves with backbeats. Notice that they are written in $\frac{6}{8}$, $\frac{9}{8}$, and $\frac{12}{8}$. These are the shuffle equivalents of $\frac{2}{4}$, $\frac{3}{4}$, and $\frac{4}{4}$ because $\frac{6}{8}$ has two groups of three per measure, $\frac{9}{8}$ has three groups of three per measure, and a measure of $\frac{12}{8}$ contains four groups of three.

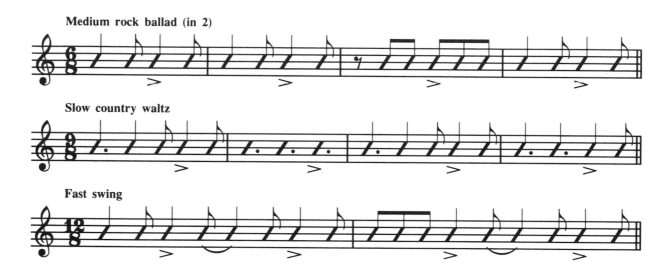

Analyze the rhythm of some of your favorite songs—or your original tunes—and determine their overall rhythmic patterns. Explore how the feel or style of each song is affected by the use of syncopation or backbeat (or the lack of it).

Songwriting Workshop

Many songwriters plan the harmony or *chord pattern* of a song first. The beat, melody, and lyrics are added later. In this section, you'll work with some basic chord patterns that have provided the foundation for many pop and rock hits. You'll create your own melody and lyrics for these time-honored patterns—and get some tips on how to handle your own chord progressions and build them into songs.

Establish the Key (I and V Chords)

The most basic harmonic structure in all popular music is made up of the I and V chords (that's the C chord and G chord in the key of C).

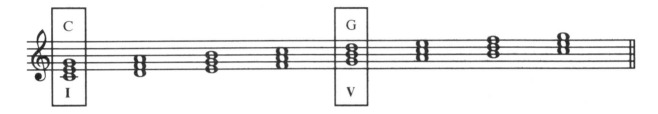

In pop, rock, blues, and jazz, the seventh is often added to the V chord to produce the *V7 chord*.

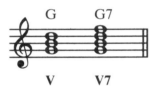

In general terms, the I chord (or *tonic*) marks the beginning and ending of a song—and the V chord (or *dominant*) provides harmonic *tension* that seeks *resolution* back to the I chord. This pattern of tension and resolution establishes the major key of a song.

Play this simple alternating I-V7 progression in the key of C using the C and G7 chords.

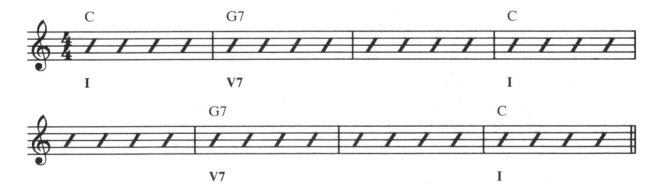

Let's take a look at how this simple harmonic pattern affects the melody of a song.

Melody and Harmony

The melody of a song naturally reflects the tension-and-release pattern of its chords. Play and sing (or just hum) the folk lullaby "Hush Little Baby." The melody sounds stable when it centers around I chord tones (1, 3, 5, and 8) and creates tension with V7 chord tones (2, 4, 5, and 7). V7-chord tension at the end of lines 1 and 3 (measures 2 and 6) causes the melody to form melodic questions. I-chord resolution at the end of lines 2 and 4 (measures 4 and 8) inspires melodic answers.

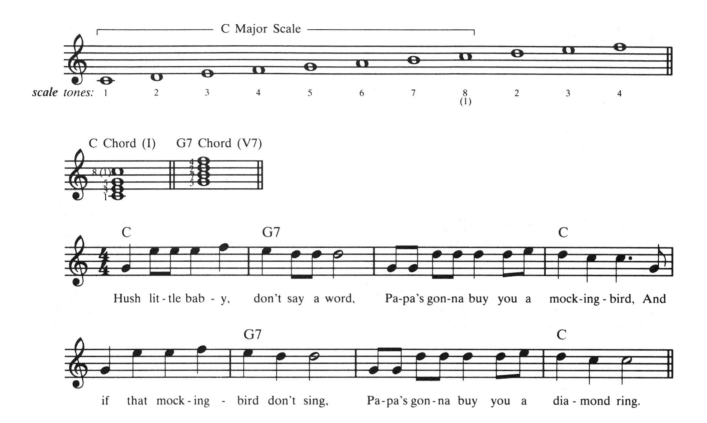

The regular rocking motion of tension and resolution of this song is the perfect musical setting for the lullaby lyric. This alternating I-V chord pattern is used in many other popular songs of yesteryear, including "Heart of My Heart" and "All I Want for Christmas (Is My Two Front Teeth)". Play and hum the melody of these old favorites—or think of another song which follows this chord pattern. Explore the shape and phrasing of each melody in terms of its simple pattern of tension and release.

Choose a Beat

Many songwriters decide on the basic beat or feel of a song early in the writing process. They use the overall rhythmic structure of the song as a framework for writing melody and lyrics. The beat often determines the style of a particular song, or the tempo. For instance, a $\frac{3}{4}$ time signature indicates waltz time, which almost always dictates a slow tune—and is commonly used in country music. Get ready to explore a few classic pop hits which use the I and V chords in different rhythmic settings. As you play each of the song settings provided below, you'll learn how different rhythmic feels add color to a simple chord pattern. You'll also get the chance to write your own melody and lyrics in these different song styles.

Rock

The classic rock song has a straightforward driving beat and predictable harmony. Melody and lyrics are correspondingly strong and simple—and often rely on repetition to create an overall sense of confidence and power.

Many rock songs use a steady $\frac{4}{4}$ rhythm with a heavy backbeat to achieve a hard-driving feel. As an example of how this solid rock feel can change a simple melody and chord pattern, take a look at "Mockingbird"—a pop/rock adaptation of "Hush, Little Baby" James Taylor and Carly Simon brought to position five on the pop charts in 1974. Gospel singer Inez Foxx also had a top-10 hit with an R&B version of this song in 1963.

Play this simple chord progression in a slow $\frac{4}{4}$ rock tempo, as indicated.

Style: Slow $\frac{4}{4}$ rock: based on "Mockingbird"
Key: C Major
Chords: I and V7
           C and G7

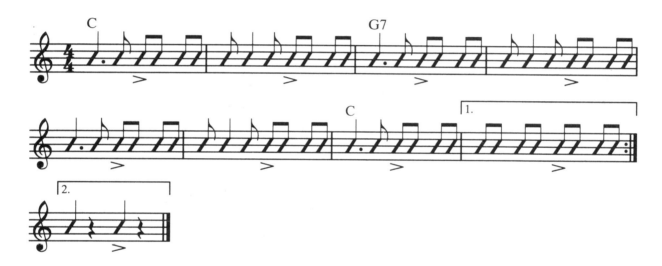

Now write your own rock melody and lyrics for this progression. Here are some guidelines.

- Shape the melody and lyric as a four-line chorus section. Repeat the progression several times as you map out the melody and lyric. Write down your ideas on music paper.
- Choose an upbeat rock theme and state the title in a musical hook. Try repeating the hook in this section—or rhyme it with another important line.
- Use an AABB or ABAB rhyme scheme. Feel free to experiment with same-word, perfect, and internal rhymes in this setting.
- Once you've completed this chorus section, try adding a verse section that leads naturally to and from the chorus in an ABAB pattern. Or, create the reverse pattern: chorus-verse (BABA).

Novelty

The traditional *novelty song* featured a humorous or odd theme— and presented a memorable character, or told an interesting story. The American vaudeville stage (and its forerunner, the English music hall) fostered many of the world's great novelty songs. And, novelty songs still take an important place in today's music industries—from publishing and recording to Broadway and Hollywood. However, today, pop and rock songs with frivolous themes (such as, "Walk Like an Egyptian" and "De Do Do Do, De Da Da Da") are considered to be in the mainstream. The modern novelty song is still likely to have a whimsical theme—but it usually also features narrative or special audio effects.

Most successful novelty songs also ride the crest of the wave of a national craze. The popularity of CB radios and the language of American truckers brought C. W. McCall's "Convoy" to the top of the pop charts. "Disco Duck" poked gentle fun at the disco craze—while songs like "The Streak" and "Pac-Man Fever" rode the wave of other popular fads. Although novelty songs like Weird Al Yankovic's "Eat It" and "Another One Rides the Bus" get nationwide attention, these are only parodies of pre-existing songs.

Novelty songs often feature a high-spirited uptempo beat to match their upbeat and humorous themes. Most rely on a distinctive and memorable rhythm to capture the listener's attention or bring a smile. The beat is often borrowed from music of a previous era to lend a nostalgic or quaint quality to the song. "They're Coming to Take Me Away, Ha-Haaa!" and "I'm Henery the Eighth I Am!" both feature boisterous, old-fashioned rhythms to set the stage for their unusual lyrics.

Take a look at how the Beatles used an old-fashioned $\frac{6}{8}$ march tempo to lend a campy beat to their novelty rock song "Yellow Submarine." This clever song combined a traditional marching band sound with rock instrumentation (and lots of sound effects). "Yellow Submarine" rose to the number two position on the charts in 1966—and later inspired a popular animated movie of the same name.

Play this I-V chord progression in $\frac{6}{8}$ time.

Style: $\frac{6}{8}$ novelty rock: based on the chorus of "Yellow Submarine"
Key: C Major
Chords: I and V7
            C and G7

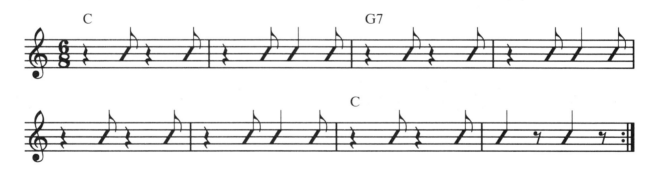

Now write your add melody and lyrics to this progression using a similar beat. Here are some suggestions.

• Form a four-line chorus section with melody and lyric.
• Choose a novel theme that centers on an unusual character, place, object, situation, or philosophy. Or, offer the listener some humorous advice.
• Feature the title in the chorus.
• Experiment with internal rhyme, multiple rhyme, and same-word rhyme. Feel free to repeat words—or give an unconventional word a place of importance. Be sure to write down your ideas.
• Once you've completed the chorus section, try writing several verse sections. These should each feature the same basic chords and melody with a new set of lyrics. Your lyric should elaborate on the unusual song theme or unravel a humorous story. Design each verse to lead naturally to and from the chorus section in this pattern: ABABAB.

The V-I Cadence

The I and V chords not only establish the key of a given song, they form an important chord pairing (V-I) called an *authentic cadence*. The authentic cadence marks the end of important phrases, song sections, and often forms the ending of a song. This classic arrangement of the I and V7 chords features a prominent authentic cadence at its end. This pattern occurs in many folk songs, including "Tom Dooley," "Bill Bailey," "Clementine," "La Cucaracha," and "Polly Wolly Doodle." As you play the pattern in tempo, sing or hum "Bill Bailey" (or another of these folk songs) in the key of G. Note how the melody centers around G chord tones and D7 chord tones, respectively.

This traditional chord pattern is used in several classic pop hits. In the next sections, you'll get a chance to create song melodies and lyrics in different styles using this chord pattern.

Easy Pop

In general terms, pop music is any type of music that is popular with the mainstream of music listeners. However, in the past few decades, pop music has developed into a distinct musical style, characterized by important vocals, pleasing harmonies, and bright electronic instrumentation. Today's pop music may be divided into two important categories: easy pop and pop/rock. Let's look at easy pop first.

The music industry has many names for easy pop music. It's sometimes called "middle-of-the-road" music or adult-oriented rock. Easy pop songs feature clear vocals and vocal harmony—and a universally important theme like love, celebration, or loneliness. Any song with these qualities, that does not feature an intense or jarring rock beat may be considered to be in the easy pop category. Pop music often features a steady $\frac{4}{4}$ beat and short, even phrases. Most easy pop songs feature a slow to medium tempo, balanced structure, clear rhyme scheme, and important hook.

Here's the I-V chord progression from "Bill Bailey" used in a pop setting. This easy feel is based on a traditional polka rhythm with strong stress on beats 1 and 3. Bobby Vinton used this simple, effective setting for his "Melody of Love," which went to number three position on the pop charts in 1974. Play this progression at a moderate tempo with the indicated pop feel.

Style: Easy pop: based on "Melody of Love"
Key: C Major
Chords: I and V7
           C and G7

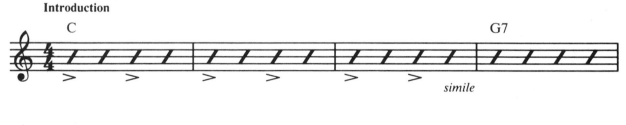

Now write your own easy pop melody and lyric in this setting using these guidelines.

- Allow an eight-bar introduction to establish the pop feel.
- Plan your chorus in four even lines. Repeat the progression several times as you explore the possibilities for melody and lyric. Jot down your ideas on music paper.

- Choose a general theme that communicates a universal message about romance or lifestyle. Or, describe a meaningful character and setting that everyone can relate to (as in "Up on the Roof" or "The Wind Beneath My Wings").
- Feature the title in the chorus as a hook. Rhyme the hook line with another line and/or repeat the hook during the chorus.
- Once you've completed the chorus section, take the time to write it out in lead-sheet form. You may then want to add a verse or bridge that develops the song theme—and leads nicely to and from the chorus.

Pop/Rock

Most of today's pop music features a driving rock beat—and bold electronic band instrumentation. Pop/rock themes tend to be more controversial than those of easy pop songs—and often appeal to a younger, more liberal-minded audience. Pop/rock superstars like Madonna, Michael Jackson, and Billy Joel speak to the majority of today's pop listeners.

Pop music typically features a steady $\frac{4}{4}$ rhythm, with equal stress on each beat. The melody and lyric should be snappy and relatively simple, with a strong and regular rhyme scheme. Add a rock beat and some flashy band instrumentation and you've got pop/rock. Try playing the pop/rock progression used in the rhythmic pop song "Take a Chance on Me," which the Swedish vocal group Abba brought to number three position in 1978.

Style: Pop/rock: based on "Take a Chance on Me"
Key: C Major
Chords: I and V7
            C and G7

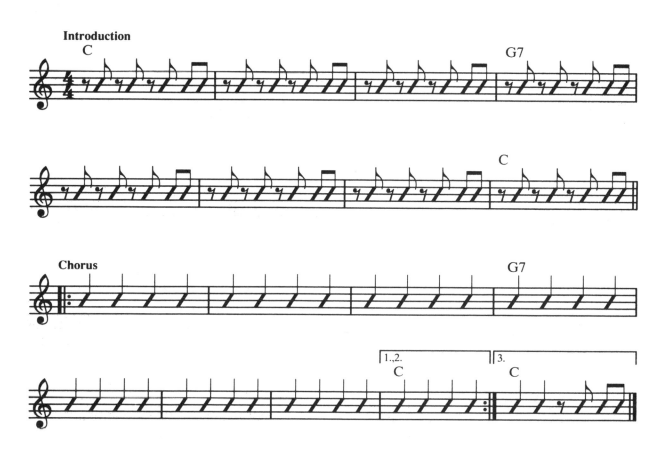

Once you are familiar with this progression, try writing your own contemporary rock chorus in this setting. Here are some guidelines.

- Allow an eight-bar instrumental introduction to establish the $\frac{4}{4}$ pop/rock beat.
- Craft your melody and lyric into an eight-line chorus section. Repeat the chorus section several times as you map out these lines.
- Choose an active theme—like dancing or falling in love—to match the insistent upbeat tempo. Summarize the theme in a one-line song hook.
- Feature the hook line in the chorus. In "Take a Chance on Me," the hook occurs in the fourth line. Try putting your hook in the fourth and eighth lines—or in the first and fourth.
- Experiment with simple perfect rhymes. Consider rhyming the hook line with another important line. Plan the rhyme scheme of the chorus in an AABBAABB pattern (or use ABCCABCC or ABABCBCB).
- Once you've completed the chorus section, create a verse section or bridge for this song. A verse should include details that help prepare the theme as stated in the chorus. A bridge should create harmonic contrast and provide a new angle on the theme.

Workshop Song 1: Uptempo Pop

Now write an up-to-date pop melody and lyric using this chord pattern and rhythm. Shape the chorus in four even phrases (or use eight short phrases). Play through this progression several times as you explore the possibilities for a theme, title, and hook for your song chorus. Experiment with melodic question and answer, melodic contour, and rhyme scheme (and write down your ideas while you are working). Once you've mapped out the melody and lyric, make a lead sheet of your song chorus—and memorize it.

You may be inspired to add a verse or bridge to the song right away—or set it aside for another session. While it's important to have regular songwriting sessions, many successful songwriters claim to have their best ideas when they're just walking down the street or sitting in a restaurant. If you keep your song ideas in mind, it's possible to work on them whenever you have a spare moment. A flash of inspiration will come when you least expect it—so be ready to jot it down. First, get familiar with this simple progression.

Style: Dance rock
Key: C Major
Chords: I and V7
            C and G7

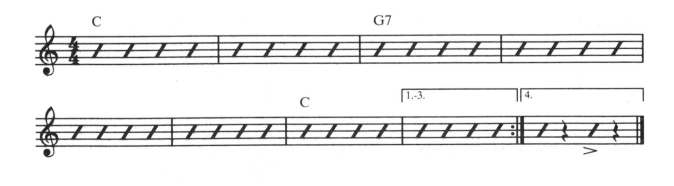

Now write your own melody and lyric in this setting. Here are some guidelines.

- Shape your chorus in four or eight lines. Or, use six phrases in this pattern: short-short-long, short-short-long. Repeat the progression as you map out the melody and lyric.
- Choose a theme that suggests movement—like celebration, driving, dancing, or loving.
- Consider placing the hook in every other line of the chorus.
- Experiment with double rhymes and internal rhymes. Plan a symmetrical rhyming pattern (like ABAB) for a four-line chorus. Also consider a tight-knit rhyme scheme (like ABACABAC) if you've chosen to write an eight-line chorus.
- Once you've completed the chorus section, you may feel inspired to write a verse or bridge for this song—or set the lead sheet aside for a later session.

The IV Chord

Like the I and V chords, the IV chord is a major triad. The IV chord is built on the fourth step of the scale (in the key of C, it's the F chord).

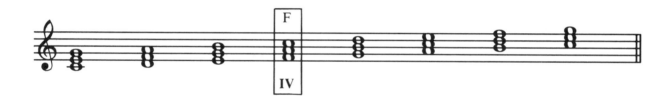

The IV-I Cadence

The song sections you've written so far feature the authentic cadence (V-I). Now compare this cadence with the sound of IV-I chord movement, called a *plagal cadence*. This harmony is perhaps best recognized as the traditional "amen" at the end of a hymn.

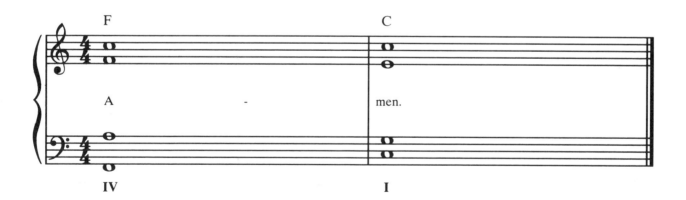

The chord progression that follows features the authentic cadence (V-I) alternating with the plagal cadence (IV-1). This pattern occurs in many American folk songs (including "Pick a Bail of Cotton," "Sourwood Mountain," and "Cripple Creek"). Hum or sing "Cripple Creek" (or another of these folk songs) as you play through the progression in tempo. Notice how the alternating cadences support the question-and-answer pattern of the melody and lyric.

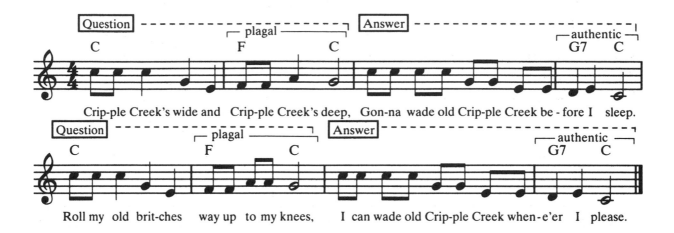

This traditional chord pattern is used in several classic pop hits—particularly those with a country flavor. In the next sections, you'll get a chance to create song melodies and lyrics in several different styles using this chord pattern and its variations.

Country/Pop

A good number of country songs have made it on the pop charts. These are called "crossover" hits—or country/pop songs. Artists like Linda Rondstadt, Dolly Parton, Kenny Rogers, and Willie Nelson have had some notable country/pop hits. Some say that's because there's a little place in the heart of every listener for the traditional music of his or her homeland.

Country music grew of out the folk dances and songs of nineteenth century rural America—particularly in the South and West. Country draws its influence from a variety of musical forms popular during this period—including the fiddle tune, folk ballad, traditional hymn, Black spiritual, and the blues. After the turn of the century, country music first entered the music marketplace—which was then controlled largely by the music publishers of New York City's "Tin Pan Alley." The first commercial country songs were considered novelty numbers and were billed as cowboy songs, hillbilly music, and "honky-tonk." In the 1920s, this specialty music emerged as a distinctive musical style. During this decade, the Grand Ole Opry became the first radio show dedicated to country music—and country stars began to achieve national fame. In time, country music achieved world popularity and fostered other popular forms—including *country/swing* and, of course, *rockabilly,* an early rock and roll form.

Country music combines simple, lilting melodies and bright harmonies in a strong and regular beat. Country tunes generally sound best when they are performed with sincerity and confidence—two qualities which contribute greatly to the music's popular appeal.

Here's the "Cripple Creek" chord pattern with a typical $\frac{4}{4}$ country/pop beat. This progression occurs in Linda Rondstadt's popular recording of "Love Is a Rose." Play the progression at a moderate tempo, with a steady, even beat.

Style: Country/pop: based on "Love Is a Rose"
Key: C Major
Chords: I, IV, and V7
           C, F, and G7

Now write your own country/pop melody and lyric for this progression using these guidelines.

- Allow an eight-bar introduction to establish the country/pop feel.
- Shape the melody and lyric as a four-line verse or chorus section—or use this progression for both verse and chorus.
- Choose a romantic or celebrative theme and use honest language to make your point. This is also a perfect setting for a story song. If you choose this route, use narrative in the verse section to develop the plot. Place the hook in first or last line of the chorus—or use a repeating hook in this section to emphasize the song theme.
- Use an ABAB or AABB rhyme scheme. Feel free to create a simple internal rhyme or use two-syllable rhyme. Don't feel compelled to rhyme the hook line with another line if it holds a strong position in the chorus.

Country/Rock

Some country/pop songs use a steady rock beat. Take a look at a variation of the I-IV-V progression used in "Love Is a Rose," which showed up in another Linda Rondstadt hit, "When Will I Be Loved." This rhythmic country/rock song enjoyed two weeks in the number two position on the pop charts in 1975.

Play this new progression with a $\frac{12}{8}$ country/rock beat. Notice how this broad time signature creates a feeling of four strong beats per measure, while the shuffle rhythm keeps things moving.

Style: Country/rock: based on "When Will I Be Loved"
Key: C Major
Chords: I, IV, and V7
          C, F, and G7

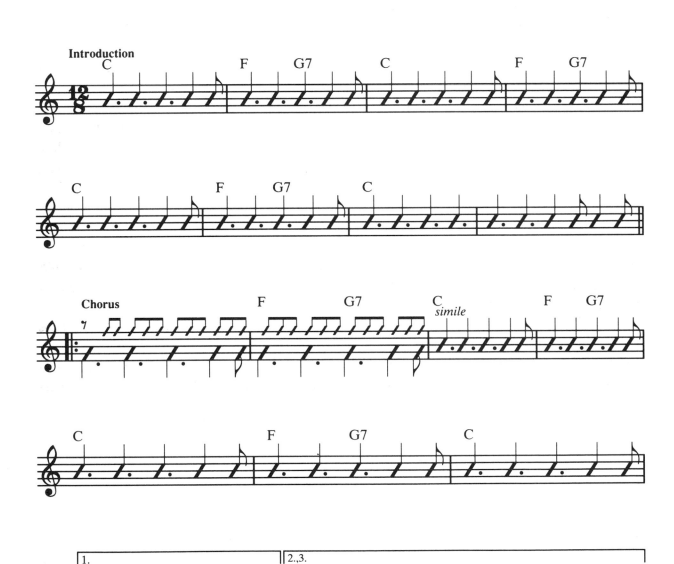

Try writing your own melody and words to this progression. Here are some suggestions.

- Allow an eight-bar introduction to establish the $\frac{12}{8}$ country/rock feel.
- Shape the melody and lyric as a four-line chorus section—with the hook in the last two lines.
- Choose a general romantic or celebrative theme. Many country/rock lyrics allow performers to explore the theme in the first person. As in "When Will I Be Loved," provide some strong emotional commitment for the singer in your lyric.
- Use an AABC rhyme scheme with the hook in the last two lines (or try an AAAB rhyme scheme). The hook line does not have to contain a rhyme in this position.

Latin Rock

Latin rhythms and melodies did much to influence jazz, pop, and rock and roll music—and have inspired many dance crazes and popular dance forms. Carlos Jobim, Ritchie Valens, Jose Feliciano, Freddie Fender, Los Lobos, Gloria Estafan, and Santana are just a few of the Latin-American artists who have brought their influence to the forefront of the pop and rock movements.

Commercial Latin rock music features a highly charged and relentless beat with lively and simple melody and lyric. Hits like "Oyo Como Va," "Conga," "La Bamba," and "Rhythm Is Gonna Get You" have earned their place as classic dance club favorites. Non-Latin artists and groups have also discovered the value of Latin influences in their music, as Madonna did with her very successful "La Isla Bonita." Your ability to create up-to-the-minute danceable Latin songs help you add flavor to many other types of rock music—especially when it comes to finding interesting and exciting rhythms.

Take a look at the lead sheet for "La Bamba." Latin rock and roll star Ritchie Valens made a hit with this song in 1959. The movie based on his life, *La Bamba*, was released in 1987—with music by the Latin-American rock quintet Los Lobos. Their version of this terrific Latin tune held the number one position on the charts for three weeks.

Play this lead sheet of "La Bamba" with the indicated Latin feel. Note that the syncopated and irregular melody of this song gives it a free-spirited and natural sound. Although the lyric is entirely in Spanish, the words are sonorous, memorable, and exciting. Your own Latin-influenced songs should have English lyrics (unless you're fluent in Spanish)—still, your lyric should capture the fluid rhythms and open sounds of spoken Spanish.

Style:	Latin rock: based on "La Bamba"
Key:	G Major
Chords:	I, IV, and V7
	G, C, and D7

La Bamba

Bam - ba, bam - ba.   Bam - ba, bam - ba.

Bam - ba, bam - ba.

The basic chord pattern of "La Bamba" is the blueprint for many other top hits—including "Twist and Shout" and "Come a Little Bit Closer," which feature strikingly similar melodies and patterns of lyric. Hum or sing one or more of these Latin-influenced melodies as you play the progression.

"Twist and Shout"   "Come a Little Bit Closer"
"Do You Love Me"   "Hang on Sloopy"
"Louie, Louie"   "Good Lovin' "

Once you've explored a few of the many hits that have used this progression, write your own Latin-influenced rock chorus using these guidelines.

- Allow an eight-bar introduction to establish the Latin feel.
- Shape the melody and lyric into a four-line chorus. Repeat the chorus harmony as you develop your ideas. Explore the possibilities for melody syncopation against the steady Latin groove.
- Choose a free-wheeling, celebrative theme that makes people want to dance.
- Don't hesitate to repeat an important word, use same-word rhymes, or give your hook center stage.

Workshop Song 2: Medium Pop/Rock

Here's an original chord pattern which uses the I, I7, IV, and V7 chords in a verse and chorus section (that's G, G7, C, and D7 in the key of G). Play this progression with the indicated pop/rock feel.

Style: Medium pop/rock ballad
Key: G Major
Chords: I, I7, IV, and V7
              G, G7, C, and D7

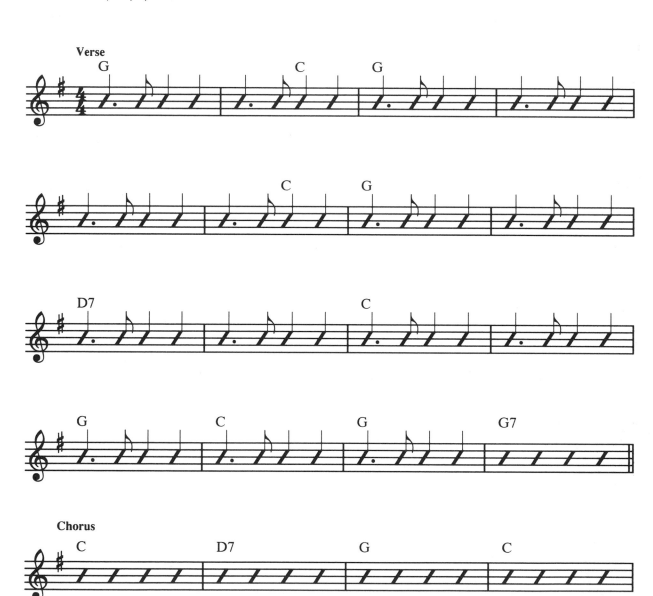

Now use this pop/rock progression as the basis for your own verse-chorus song. Here are some guidelines.

- Build a four-line verse and a four-line chorus.
- Choose a romantic, celebrative, or reflective theme.
- Develop your setting, character, or story in the verse sections. Summarize the theme in the chorus—and drive home the hook.

Minor Chords

Within a major key, certain triads naturally occur as minor chords. The next sections explore the VIm, IIm, and IIIm chords and their typical uses in a major key setting.

The VIm Chord

The *VI Minor chord* (abbreviated *VIm*) is built on the sixth step of the scale. This produces an A Minor chord in the key of C.

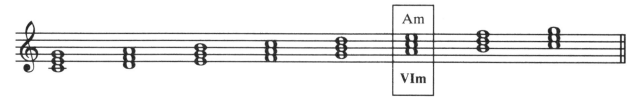

The VIm chord shares two notes in common with the I chord. This makes for smooth transitions between the two chords when used in a progression. It also means that the VIm may be used as a substitute for the I chord.

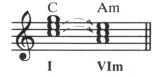

Let's explore how the VIm chord is used in some pop and rock settings.

Fifties Rock Shuffle

During the 1950s, many rhythmic slow tunes featured a ⁶⁄₈ shuffle beat. These classic hard-driving ballads include "Blueberry Hill," "Oh, Donna," "Young Love," and "The Wanderer." In its pure form, this beat is often used in commercial jingles—and in fifties revival musicals like *Grease* and *Pump Boys and Dinettes*. You'll find it's a useful beat to have under your belt—and well worth reusing in a nostalgic pop/rock song.

Play the chord progression for "Heart and Soul" in a ⁶⁄₈ shuffle pattern. This classic Hoagy Carmichael hit was remade as a doo-wop song by the Cleftones in 1961; and Jan & Dean put it on the charts in the same year.

Style: Fifties rock shuffle: based on "Heart and Soul"
Key: C Major
Chords: I, IV, V7, and VIm
          C, F, G7, and Am

Once you're familiar with this chord pattern, write your own rock shuffle melody and lyric for this progression. Here are some guidelines.

- Allow a sixteen-bar introduction to establish the shuffle feel.
- Shape the melody and lyric as a four-line chorus section.
- Choose a romantic or celebrative theme and use a simple and direct lyric to make your point.
- Use an AAAB or AABC rhyme scheme with the hook in the last line—or repeat the hook throughout the chorus.
- Once you've completed this chorus section, try adding a verse section that leads naturally to and from the chorus in an ABAB pattern.

Contemporary Pop/Rock

Pop/rock music dominates today's hit charts. Unlike the easygoing pop music of the seventies, the pop of the nineties is characterized by a driving rock beat and powerful electronic instrumentation. A relentless eighth-note groove and a big backbeat provide a strong rhythmic setting for "Every Breath You Take," which was a number-one hit for the Police for an amazing eight weeks. Play this progression at a moderate tempo with the indicated feel.

Style: Contemporary pop/rock: based on "Every Breath You Take"
Key: C Major
Chords: I, IV, V7, and VIm
           C, F, G7, and Am

Now write your own pop/rock chorus using this progression. Here are a few suggestions.

- Allow an eight-bar introduction to establish the pop/rock feel.
- Shape the melody and lyric as a four-line chorus section.
- Choose an upbeat rock theme and state the title in a musical hook. Try repeating the hook in this section—or rhyme it with another important line.
- Use an AAAB rhyme scheme with the hook in the last line. Or, try an ABCB pattern. Stick to simple single-syllable rhymes.
- Once you've completed this chorus section, try adding a verse section that leads naturally to and from the chorus in an ABAB pattern. Or, create the reverse pattern: chorus-verse (BABA).

Rhythm & Blues

In the 1930s and 1940s, Black jazz bands began to play their own hard-driving version of the blues. This new rhythmic blues music was great for dancing—and inspired many later styles, including soul, Motown, funk, and even rap.

Rhythm & blues songs often feature a slow, powerful beat and a relaxed groove. The melody and lyric are formed in short, regular phrases—and use syncopation to create a steady, hip rhythm. The lyric is direct and natural-sounding—and explores general themes, like love, survival, or celebration. Some rhythm & blues songs focus on traditional blues themes, like separation, loss, and loneliness. Strong rhymes, repeated words, and complementary sounds provide power and movement in the lyric—and add to the overall rhythmic effect of the song.

A typical rhythm & blues ballad features a moderately slow $\frac{4}{4}$ metre and a heavy backbeat. Take a look at the syncopated rhythm & blues feel used in the popular hit "Stand by Me." This terrific song has been a top-40 hit no less than five times—as recorded by Ben E. King (1961), Spyder Turner (1967), John Lennon (1975), Mickey Gilley (1980), and Ben E. King again in 1986.

Style: Rhythm & blues: based on "Stand by Me"
Key: C Major
Chords: I, IV, V7, and VIm
           C, F, G7, and Am

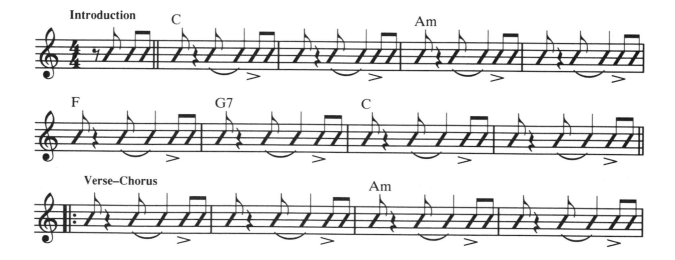

play three times

repeat and fade

After you've explored this rhythm & blues progression, try writing your own melody and lyric in this setting. Here are some suggestions:

• Allow for an eight-measure instrumental introduction to get you in the groove.
• Shape the melody and lyric as a four-line verse or chorus section ("Stand by Me" actually uses the same pattern for verse and chorus).
• Choose a strong general theme. Use natural-sounding language that is direct and to the point.
• Use an AAAB rhyme scheme with the hook in the last line. Or, try an AABB or ABCB pattern. Stick to simple single-syllable rhymes.

The IIm Chord

The *II Minor chord* (abbreviated *IIm*) is built on the second step of the major scale—that's the Dm chord in the key of C.

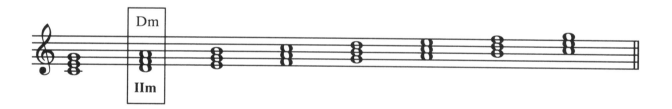

The IIm chord naturally leads to the V chord (which then leads to the I chord). This IIm-V-I progression occurs frequently in pop, rock, and jazz music—and may be considered an extended version of the V-I authentic cadence.

Fifties Straight-Eighth Pop

Take a look at a variation of the chord pattern used in "Stand by Me" and "Every Breath You Take." Here, the IIm chord is used in place of the IV chord. This model is based on the fifties classic "All I Have to Do Is Dream," which was a number one hit for the Everly Brothers in 1958. Play this progression with the indicated fifties pop feel.

Style: Fifties straight-eighth pop: based on "All I Have to Do Is Dream"
Key: C Major
Chords: I, IIm, V7, and VIm
           C, Dm, G7, and Am

Introduction

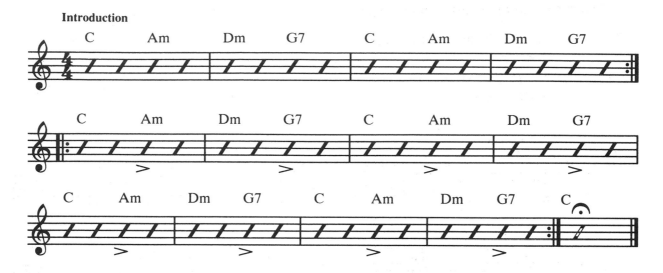

Once you are familiar with this progression, try writing your own straight-eighth ballad in this setting. Here are some guidelines.

• Allow an eight-bar instrumental introduction to establish the   straight-eighth groove.
• Choose a theme that takes a positive view of romance or lifestyle—and capture the theme in the title/ hook.
• Experiment with internal rhyme, as well as perfect and imperfect rhyme to create a balanced and catchy lyric.
• Once you've completed the chorus section, try adding a verse or bridge to the song.

The IIIm Chord

The triad built on the third step of the scale is called *III Minor* (abbreviated *IIIm*).

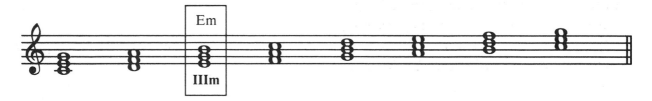

The IIIm chord shares two common tones with the I chord—and often follows the I chord in a stepwise progression.

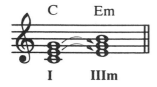

Contemporary Straight-Eighth Rock

Many contemporary rock songs still contain elements of early rockabilly music. Take a look at the IIIm chord as used in Elton John's "Crocodile Rock" (which was a number one hit on the pop charts for three weeks in 1972).

Play this A Major progression with an up-tempo straight-eighth rock rhythm.

Style: Straight-eighth rock: based on "Crocodile Rock"
Key: A Major
Chords: I, IIIm, IV, and V7
             A, C♯m, D, and E7

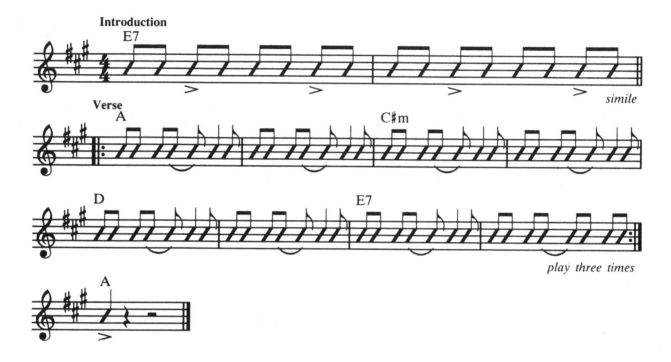

Now write your own song verse in this setting using these guidelines.

- Allow a two-bar instrumental introduction to establish the straight-eighth groove.
- Choose an upbeat theme that celebrates dance, music, or love.
- Use an AABB or ABAB rhyme scheme. Feel free to use perfect and strong imperfect rhyme. You may also want to have an internal rhyme to tie the verse together.
- Once you've completed the verse, add a chorus section. Then write additional lyrics for two more verses and put the song together in an ABABAB pattern.

Workshop Song 3: Pop/Rock Ballad

Here's an interesting chord progression that uses all of the basic minor chords in the key of C Major. The verse section is based on the 1961 Elvis Presley hit "Can't Help Falling in Love," which Corey Hart remade as a hit in 1987. The bridge is based on an extended version of the bridge section in Bette Midler's "The Rose."

Note that this progression uses a C chord with a G note in the bass (abbreviated *C/G*) which creates a great stepwise bass pattern at the beginning of the verse. Play this progression with the indicated $\frac{4}{4}$ pop feel.

Style: Pop/rock ballad: based on "Can't Help Falling in Love" and "The Rose"
Key: C Major
Chords: I, I/V, IIm, IIIm, IV, V7, and VIm
           C, C/G, Dm, Em, F, G7, and Am

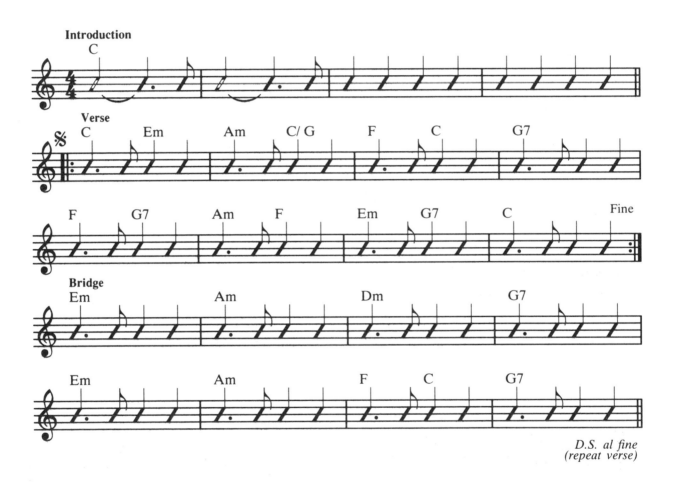

D.S. al fine
(repeat verse)

Now create your own pop ballad using this harmonic setting. Here are some suggestions.

• Allow a four-bar instrumental introduction to get you into the pop feel.
• Plan for a four-line verse and a four-line bridge section in an AABA pattern.
• Choose a reflective or romantic theme to correspond with the easygoing tempo.
• Use an ABAB or ABCB rhyme scheme in the verse and bridge. Craft the melody and lyric of the bridge to provide contrast to the verse—but be sure it leads smoothly back to the verse and works to support your overall song theme.

Chords Outside the Key

Certain chords that occur outside a major key may be used in a major setting because of their strong relationship to chords within the key. The next sections explore the II7, III7, VI7, and ♭VII chords and their typical functions in a major key setting.

The II7 Chord

The II7 chord in the key of C Major is the D7 chord. The F♯ note in this chord is called an *accidental* in this context, because it occurs outside the key of C Major.

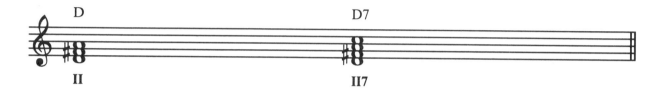

This D Major chord may be used in a C Major song, however, because it acts as the V chord of the V chord (that is, the V of the G chord) and implies the related key of G Major.

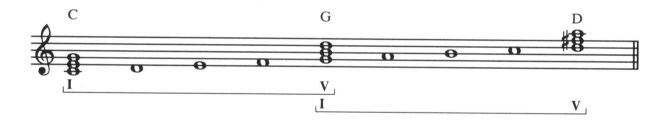

In this way, the II7 leads naturally to the V7 chord, and the V7 to I.

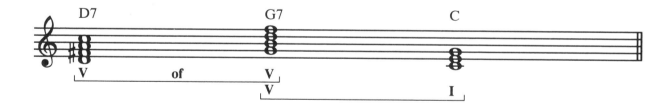

Like the IIm-V-I progression you worked with earlier, the II7-V7-I pattern occurs frequently in pop and rock music—and may be considered an extended version of the authentic cadence (V-I).

Take a look at the lead sheet for the traditional American cowboy song, "Red River Valley" in the key of F Major. This song features the II7 chord (G7) in a typical progression. Hum or sing "Red River Valley" as you play through the song in tempo. Notice how the two-line question phrase of the melody ends with a II7-V cadence (that's V-I in the key of C) and the answer ends with a V-I in the home key of F.

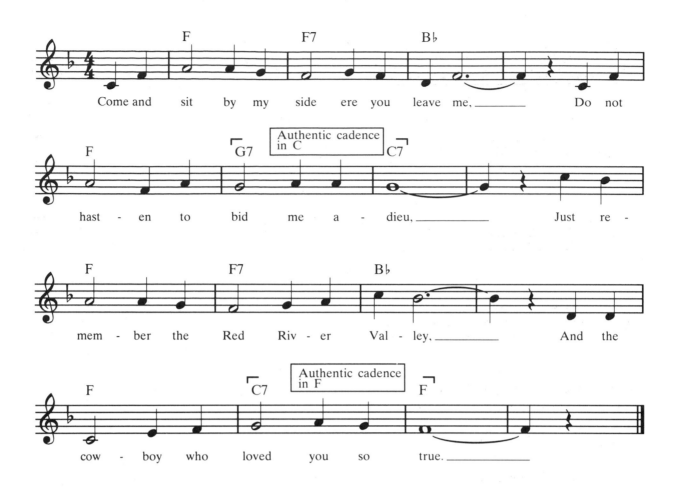

Come and sit by my side ere you leave me,_____ Do not
hast - en to bid me a - dieu,_____ Just re -

Authentic cadence in C

mem - ber the Red Riv - er Val - ley,_____ And the

Authentic cadence in F

cow - boy who loved you so true._____

This traditional chord pattern is used in several classic rock songs—particularly those with a down-and-dirty sound (as you will see in the next section).

Medium Hard-Rock

Hard rock music began in the 1960s, and came to a head in the early 1970s. This style of music is characterized by heavy guitar instrumentation, powerful vocals, and a hard-driving rock beat. Bands like the Rolling Stones, the Grateful Dead, and Led Zeppelin pioneered this hard-edged sound, which remains popular among rock fans today.

The chord progression used in "Red River Valley" occurs in several classic rock hits, including the Rolling Stones' "Honky Tonk Women," which was a number one hit for four weeks in 1969. Like "Red River Valley," the lyric and harmony of this song evoke a distinctly country-western flavor. The beat and melody, however, are quintessential rock and roll. Play the progression at a moderate tempo.

Style:	Medium hard-rock: based on "Honky Tonk Women"
Key:	F Major
Chords:	I, I7, II7, IV, and V7
	F, F7, G7, Bb, and G7

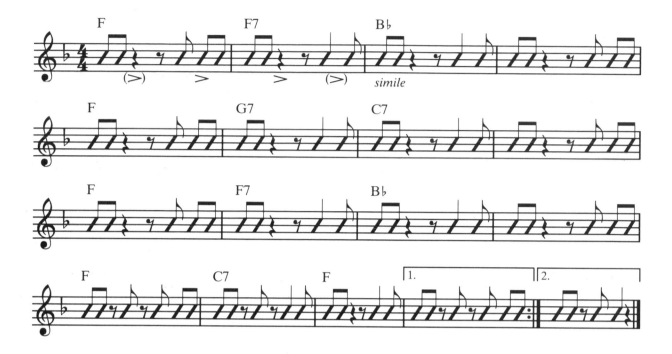

Once you are familiar with this progression, write your own hard rock verse section in this setting. Here are some suggestions.

- Shape melody and lyric in a four-line verse section.
- Choose an earthy, active theme that focuses on a gritty character, setting, or life philosophy. Driving, loving, breaking up, and listening to rock music are typical hard rock themes. Details in your lyric will help to paint the overall portrait of hard living and hard loving so characteristic of this musical style.
- Use an ABCB rhyme scheme in your verse—or the stricter ABAB scheme, if appropriate. Feel free to craft perfect or strong imperfect one-syllable rhymes. Keep the language simple and honest.
- You may wish to add a chorus section once you've completed the verse. Be sure to create a neat lead sheet at the end of your session that is easy to refer to later.

Workshop Song 4: Rock Dance

Here's a contemporary chord progression in C Major that incorporates the II7 chord in an interesting way. In the verse section, the repeated I-II7 pattern is used to create mounting tension, which is not resolved until the first chord of the chorus. In this way, the entire verse functions as a question, while the chorus provides the answer.

In the chorus, the II7 chord moves typically to the V chord, but the song never resolves to the I chord, it simply fades out. This leaves the listener with a feeling of excitement (and even anticipation) after the song has ended—a perfect mood to create on today's crowded dance floor.

Play this progression with the indicated rock feel.

Style: Rock dance
Key: C Major
Chords: I, II7, IV, and V7
            C, D7, F, and G7

Now create your own pop ballad using this harmonic setting. Here are some suggestions.

- Allow an eight-bar instrumental introduction to get you into the rock groove.
- Plan the melody and lyric in two sixteen-bar verses, followed by a sixteen-bar chorus. Use the introduction for an instrumental break, then repeat the verse-verse-chorus pattern—and fade out as you repeat the chorus.
- Choose an upbeat, celebrative theme to correspond with the song's exciting, danceable rhythm. Or, select a darker theme that focuses on danger or a stormy romance.
- Try using an AAAB rhyme scheme for the verse sections—and an ABAB scheme in the chorus. (Or, you may want to reserve the chorus for repetition of the hook line in an AAAB pattern.)

The III7 and VI7 Chords

The III7 and VI7 chords are major versions of IIIm and VIm, built on the third and sixth degrees of the scale, respectively.

As you know, the II chord does not occur naturally in a major key—but it has a strong relationship to the V chord as "V of V," suggesting the key of the V chord—G Major in the key of C. In the same way, the VI chord acts as "V of II" to suggest the key of D Major—and the III chord acts as "V of VI," suggesting the key of A Major. This pattern is called the *circle of fifths*—and the chords in this cycle are used by songwriters to add dimension and fullness the harmony of a song.

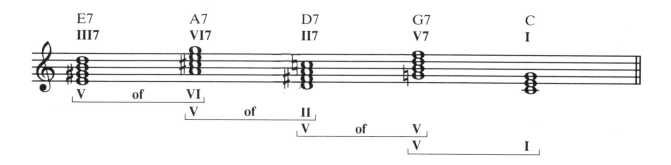

Let's look at some of the typical functions of these chords in popular song settings.

Country Waltz

Take a look at the chord progression of "The Tennessee Waltz," which is noted here in the key of G. This song incorporates many of the chords you've worked with in previous sections—as well as the III7 and VI7 chords. Although many waltzes are noted in $\frac{3}{4}$ time, this version uses $\frac{9}{8}$ time to achieve a shuffle waltz feel. Play the progression in tempo and compare the use of major and minor chords (IIm and VIm are used in the verse sections, while II7 and VI7 occur in the bridge).

Style: Country waltz: based on "The Tennessee Waltz"
Key: G Major
Chords: I, I7, IIm, II7, III7, IV, V7, VIm, and VI7
             G, G7, Am, A7, B7, C, D7, Em, and E7

Once you've practiced this progression, try writing your own waltz song in this harmonic setting. Here are some guidelines.

- Allow a four-bar instrumental introduction to establish the shuffle waltz feel.
- Plan the melody and lyric in an AABA song structure (that's verse-verse-bridge-verse). Note the variation in the cadential harmony of the first verse, as compared with verses 2 and 3.
- Choose a reflective, nostalgic, or romantic theme to complement the sweet and easy waltz rhythm.
- Rhyme the last line of each verse section, as in "The Tennessee Waltz." Try creating an imperfect rhyme for the second line of each of these verses. You may also wish to rhyme the last line of the chorus with the last line of the final verse (which is a great place for the hook).

Workshop Song 5: Jazzy Show Tune

Jazz standards and Broadway show tunes traditionally incorporate chords in the circle of fifths to create dramatic and full harmonic movement. Since the major chords outside the key suggest relationships to other major keys, they add an overall feeling of grandness and color to a song. These qualities are perfect for the stage, where full orchestrations and dramatic delivery justify the broad harmonic setting.

Here's an up-tempo show-tune progression with a ragtime feel that incorporates chords within the circle of fifths. The $\frac{12}{8}$ shuffle feel gives the pattern a jaunty, carefree character that practically begs for a clever melody and lyric. Practice the chord progression in tempo.

Style: Ragtime show tune
Key: C Major
Chords: I, II7, III7, IV7, V7, and VI7
        C, D7, E7, F7, G7, and A7

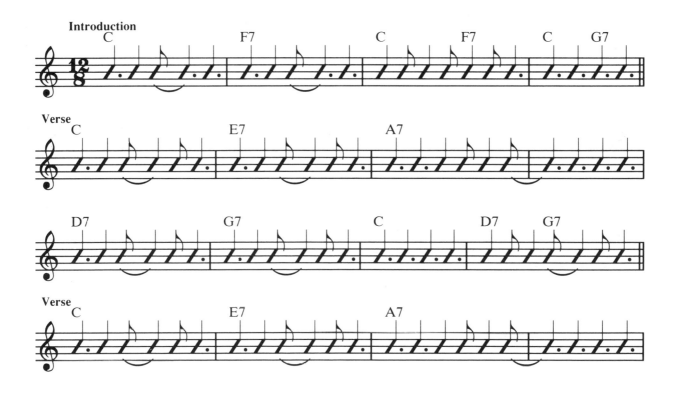

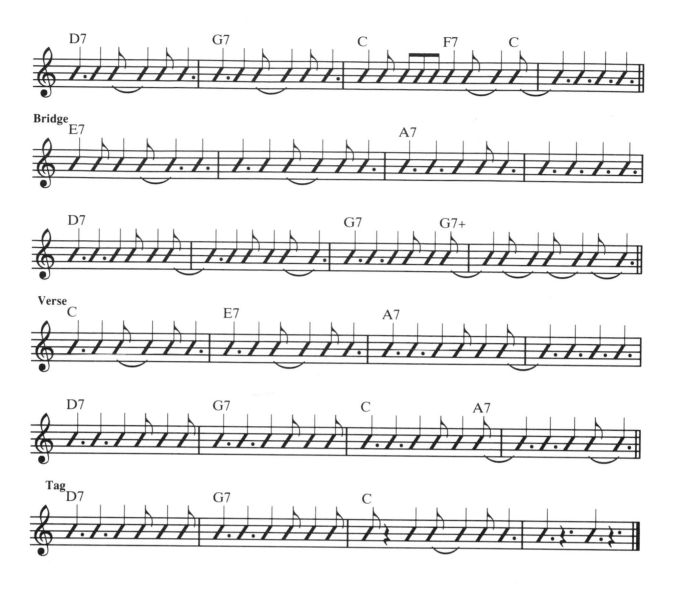

Now create your own show-tune verse in this harmonic setting. Here are some guidelines.

- Allow a four-bar instrumental introduction establish the $\frac{12}{8}$ shuffle feel.
- Craft the melody and lyric in an AABA song structure (that's verse-verse-bridge-verse). Note the harmonic variation at the end of each verse section.
- Allow two extended phrases in each verse. Place the hook in the last line of the final verse—and repeat it in the traditional tag at the end.
- Choose an upbeat or celebrative theme to complement the song's broad and cheerful rhythm. You may even wish to make the song a full-fledged novelty number by choosing a cleverly outlandish theme—and working in the hook as an opening line and punch line.
- Rhyme the two lines in each of the first two verse sections (AA then BB)—or use an ABAB rhyme scheme to link the first two verses. Try an ABCB rhyme scheme in the bridge. Feel free to explore internal rhyme and multiple rhymes—especially as comic elements in the lyric.

The ♭VII Chord

The ♭VII chord is another important chord that may be used to write songs in a major key. Even its root tone, the B♭ note, occurs outside the C Major scale.

This B♭ chord seems appropriate in a C Major setting because it acts as a IV chord (B♭) to the IV chord (F) in the key of C. Thus, the ♭VII chord is sometimes called *IV of IV,* and suggests the nearby key of F Major.

The ♭VII chord also occurs in rock music as a substitute for the V7 chord. In this context it is used to build tension and imply a minor modality when the more usual V7 chord is expected. Notice the two tones shared by these similar chords.

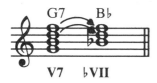

Let's take a look at both functions of the ♭VII chord in a G Major rock song setting.

Medium Pop/Rock

The progression that follows is based on the Beatles' song "You've Got to Hide Your Love Away." This pattern incorporates the ♭VII chord in a medium ⁴⁄₄ tempo with a strong backbeat on 2 and 4. As you play the progression in the key of G, note that the ♭VII chord (F) functions as the IV of IV (C) in measures 4 and 8 of the verse section. In measures 2 and 6, the ♭VII chord serves its other function as a V7 chord substitute.

Style: Medium pop/rock: based on ''You've Got to Hide Your Love Away''
Key: G Major
Chords: I, IV, V, V7, and ♭VII
G, C, D, D7, and F

Now write your own rock melody and lyric in this setting, using these guidelines.

- Allow a four-bar instrumental introduction to establish the $\frac{4}{4}$ rock beat.
- Shape the melody and lyric in a ten-bar verse section with two extended phrases, using an AA rhyme scheme. The last two measures of the verse section are really just tacked on to provide harmonic transition back to the beginning of the verse, or into the chorus.
- Craft a three-line chorus with the hook repeated in each line. The instrumental tag simply provides the harmonic resolution needed to end the song.
- Choose a romantic or reflective theme—and select a title/hook that fits nicely in the chorus section.

Workshop Song 6: New Wave

New wave music began in the late 1970s with groups like Blondie, the Cars, and the Police. This exciting new form of pop/rock incorporated a punky danceable sound with clever themes and lyrics. New wave also helped bring other world musics to the pop scene, including the reggae and West African sounds. Today, the new wave influence is clear in the work of various groups, including U2, Pet Shop Boys, and the Bangles.

Check out this rock dance progression, which uses the ♭VII chord frequently as a V7 chord substitute. This creates an electrifying, new-wave flavor that is energetic and danceable. Play this verse-chorus rock progression in tempo.

Style: New wave
Key: C Major
Chords: I, IIm, IV, V7, VIm, and ♭VII
            C, Dm, F, G7, Am, and B♭

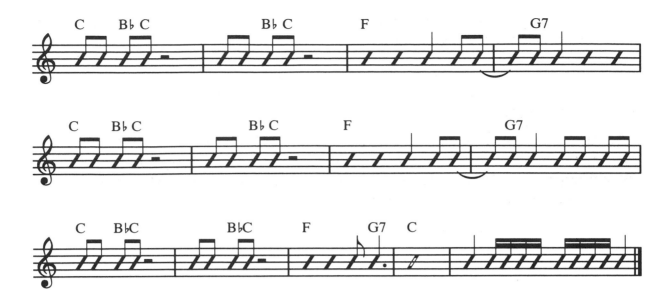

Now create your own new wave melody and lyric in this setting. Here are some suggestions.

- Allow a four-bar instrumental introduction to get in the moderate dance groove.
- Shape the melody and lyric in a four-line verse section, followed by a four-line chorus (the last measure of the chorus is an instrumental ending).
- Choose a hip theme that celebrates modern living or put an interesting twist on a modern emotional problem or desire.
- Short phrases, snappy lyrics, and syncopation will bring out the best in this interesting harmonic setting.
- Choose an active and celebrative theme—or pick a sexy or dangerous theme that complements the tension of the song's harmony and rhythm.
- Use an AAAB rhyme scheme in the verse. Repeat the hook line in the chorus.

Minor Keys

A minor key lends a special tonal color, or *tonality,* to a piece. In most cases, the minor key is used to create an introspective, sad, or hard quality in a song. This section explores the different minor keys and how they are formed. Notice that the third, sixth, and seventh notes of the minor scale are lowered by one half-step, as compared to a major scale.

In order to avoid the routine writing of the accidentals, music written in the key of C Minor features a key signature with three flats (like the key of E♭ Major). This brings the need for accidentals to a minimum.

Relative and Parallel Minor

Because the key of C Minor uses the same key signature as E♭ Major, it is known as the *relative minor* of this major key. Correspondingly, the key of E♭ Major is known as the *relative major* of C Minor. Here's a list of all major keys and their relative minors. Notice that the relative major key is always three half-steps (a minor third) up from the note named by the corresponding minor key.

Major Key	Relative Minor Key
C	A Minor
G	E Minor
D	B Minor
A	F♯ Minor
E	C♯ Minor
B	G♯ Minor
F♯	D♯ Minor
C♯	A♯ Minor
F	D Minor
B♭	G Minor
E♭	C Minor
A♭	F Minor
D♭	B♭ Minor
G♭	E♭ Minor
C♭	A♭ Minor

Since the C Minor scale uses the same starting note as the key of C Major, it is called the *tonic minor* of this major key. For this same reason, C Major and C Minor are also sometimes called *parallel keys*. Many minor songs contain elements of a major key to provide contrast and movement. Compare some of the important major and minor variations of the C chord.

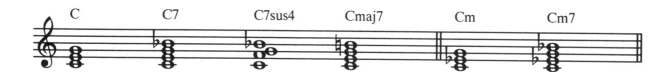

In the sections that follow, you'll see how major chords may be used selectively to provide contrast and movement in a minor song harmony (in much the same way that minor chords are used in major-key songs). This is particularly true of the V chord, which may have both major and minor qualities during the course of a song. In the workshop song at the end of this section, you'll get a chance to create a song that uses key change (or *modulation*) to change from one minor key to another.

Disco

Disco came on the scene in the 1970s, and enjoyed great popularity as a dance form until the early 1980s. The relentless pulsing beat of disco hits like "Stayin' Alive" and "The Hustle" brought America to its feet. Although the disco craze was over by the mid-eighties, its musical elements are alive and well in today's rock and pop music. In fact, many current groups have updated the disco style—and given it a new place on the dance floor.

Take a look at the minor progression used in "Bad Girls," which was a number one hit for Donna Summer for five weeks in 1979. The minor mode gives this song a hard edge that really brings out the theme. Note how the V7 chord in the last measure of the bridge provides a brighter major harmony in contrast to the minor sound of the verse and chorus.

Style: Disco: based on "Bad Girls"
Key: C Minor
Chords: Im, IVm7, Vm7, V7sus4, V7, and VImaj7
            Cm, Fm7, Gm7, G7sus4, G7, and A♭maj7

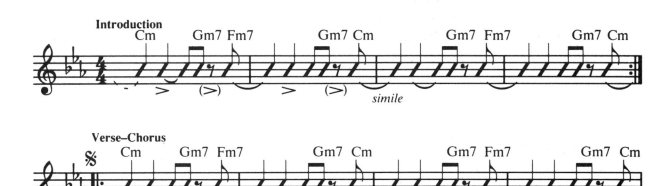

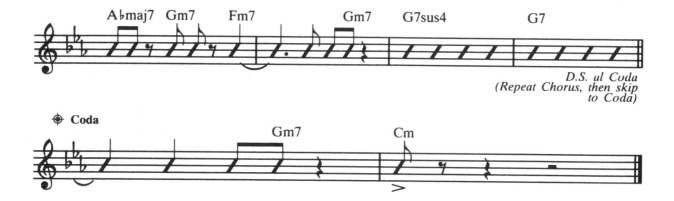

D.S. al Coda
(Repeat Chorus, then skip to Coda)

Once you are familiar with this pattern, create your own melody and lyric in this setting. Here are some guidelines.

- Allow an eight-bar instrumental introduction to establish the disco beat.
- Shape the melody and lyric in a four-line verse section, followed by a four-line chorus. The verse and chorus each use the same chord progression. Try using extended multisyllable phrases in the verse section (as in a rap song). Use shorter simpler phrases in the chorus—and drive home the hook.
- Use an ABAB rhyme scheme in the verse. Repeat the hook line in the chorus, as well as in the tag line.
- Choose an active theme that suggests power and movement—like dancing, driving, working, or making love.

Hard Rock Ballad

A rock ballad or "power ballad" is a slow-to-moderate song with a broad rock beat. Most rock ballads feature sustained notes and dramatic phrasing—and center on themes of romance or lifestyle philosophy. Rock ballads work well in a minor setting—as their typically serious and emotional themes are complemented by dark minor harmonies.

Take a look at this lead sheet for "House of the Rising Sun," which was a number one hit for the Animals in 1964. Frijid Pink put this hard-driving rock ballad on the charts again for eleven weeks in 1970. The minor mode gives "House of the Rising Sun" a bluesy rock sound and adds power to the tragic story told in the lyrics. As you play this song, notice how the melody uses the natural minor scale until the authentic cadence at the end (V7-Im). This suggestion of the major scale provides interest and contrast in this moving song.

Style: Hard rock ballad: "House of the Rising Sun"
Key: F Minor
Chords: Im, III, IV, V7sus4, V7, and VI
           Fm, A♭, B♭, C7sus4, C7, and D♭

2. My mother was a tailor,
   She sewed my new blue jeans.
   My father was a gambling man,
   Way down in New Orleans.

3. Oh, mother, tell your children,
   Not to do what I have done;
   To live in sin and misery,
   In the House of the Rising Sun.

4. *Repeat first verse*

Workshop Song 7: Minor Pop Ballad

Here's a pop progression that begins in A Minor, then modulates to E Minor for the chorus section. Although some songs use harmonic modulation to provide for an exciting arrangement—here, the modulation is an integral part of the song itself. Exploring two different keys provides for a bold contrast between the verse and the chorus. The keys used here (A Minor and E Minor) have a strong relationship to one another, for E is the dominant (or V) of A, and A is the sub-dominant (or IV) of E. These relationships make for smooth and strong movement from one key to another during modulation. Major chords are used in this progression to provide additional harmonic interest. The interesting VI7 chord in measure twelve of the verse section is not common to either minor key used in the song. Note the bluesy effect that this chord creates in the song.

Play through this basic verse-chorus pattern. Allow one verse of instrumental introduction before the song begins. The final chorus leads to a brief *coda* or tag.

Style: Minor pop ballad
Key: A Minor/E Minor
Chords: A Minor: Im, IVm, Vm, V7, VI, VI7, and VII
           Am, Dm, Em, E7, F, F7, and G
           E Minor: Im, I7, III, V7, and VI
           Em, E7, G, B7, and C

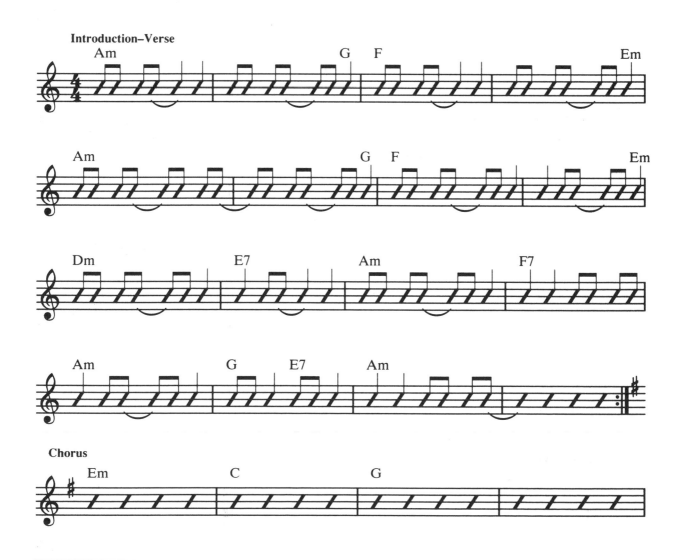

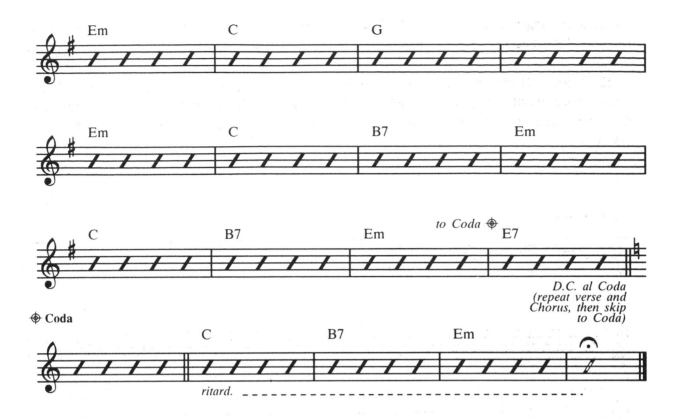

- Allow a sixteen bar instrumental introduction to establish the key and feel.
- Shape the melody and lyric in a four-line verse section, followed by a four-line chorus. The progression ends with a four measure instrumental tag—or you could repeat the last line of the chorus as a hook during the tag.
- Use an ABAB or AABB rhyme scheme in the verse. Repeat the hook line in the chorus—or follow an AAAB rhyme scheme with the hook in the last line.
- Choose an introspective or sad theme to complement the slow tempo and minor sound. Provide a new angle on the theme during the chorus section to correspond with the new harmonic setting.

The Blues

Early rock and roll borrowed heavily from the blues. In fact, many hits by Chuck Berry, Elvis Presley, and Little Richard were nothing more than blues songs with a rock and roll beat. "Hound Dog," "Good Golly, Miss Molly," "Maybelline," "Blue Suede Shoes," "Kansas City," "Tutti Frutti," and countless others follow the twelve-bar blues format to a tee.

In this section, you'll get some practice writing standard twelve-bar blues/rock songs. Your ability to create blues/rock songs will come in handy when writing songs in other styles. In fact, many of today's songwriters incorporate blues elements in their work—whether it's rock, pop, jazz, country, or a Broadway musical. Singer/songwriters Leon Redbone, Tom Waits, George Thoroughgood, Bonnie Raitt, Janis Joplin, and Ray Charles (just to name a few) all drew heavily on the blues to create their own personal sound.

The blues scale sounds somewhere in between major or minor—for it contains elements of both modes. It is also called the *pentatonic blues scale* because it only has five distinct notes (compared with the seven notes of the major scale). The "blue notes" are the flatted third and seventh (E♭ and B♭ in the key of C).

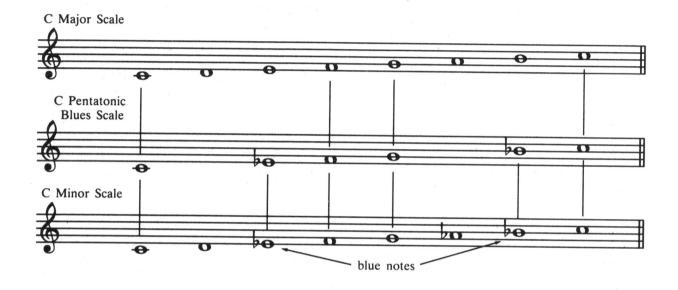

Workshop Song 8: Medium Blues/Rock

Take a look at the lead sheet for "Good Morning Blues." This chord pattern is the blueprint for all standard twelve-bar blues songs. Each verse features three lines of lyric. The first two lines are identical—and the final line rhymes with these to produce a call-and-response effect. The melody focuses on the notes of the pentatonic blues scale (except during the last phrase, where the D note provides some gritty tension). Play and hum or sing "Good Morning Blues" in the indicated blues/rock rhythm.

Style: Blues/rock: "Good Morning Blues"
Key: C Major Blues
Chords: I7, IV7, and V7
          C7, F7, and G7

Once you are familiar with "Good Morning Blues," take a look at some of the other all-time hits that have used this chord progression. Figure out the melody to any of the following hit tunes, then sing or play each familiar melody in tempo along with the "Good Morning Blues" progression.

"Hound Dog"   "Rock Around the Clock"

"Blue Suede Shoes"   "Your Mama Don't Dance"

After you've explored one or two of the previous songs, try your hand at writing your own blues/rock tune. You'll want to stick pretty closely to the pentatonic blues scale when crafting the melody. Experiment with these notes in different patterns in tempo with a twelve-bar blues progression—then shape your melody into a three-line verse.

Once you hit on a strong melody—add lyrics to your blues/rock song. Remember, a blues lyric is only powerful when it is plain and honest. Stick to expressing emotions that you understand well—and state them simply from a personal point of view. Most blues/rock lyrics focus on the human predicament—and deal with a universal problem like loneliness, lost love, or survival in a difficult world. Don't be afraid to change the rhythm of the melody somewhat from verse to verse to accommodate a changing lyric.

Further Study

The techniques and concepts you've learned in this program are designed to help you throughout your songwriting career. From this point on, you should continue to expand your creative experience by listening to, analyzing, and writing songs, songs, and more songs. Self-discipline is as important as talent when it comes to songwriting—so, schedule regular writing sessions, set reasonable goals, and write down all your ideas on music paper. Keep one copy of each of your original songs in a folder for easy reference. Store another copy in a different area of your home or studio for safekeeping.

There are many things you can do to learn more about your craft and advance your songwriting career. Get involved with other songwriters and musicians who are active in their field. Listen to the work of other new songwriters and seek advice from writers who have more experience than you. Create opportunities for your song to be performed. Consider recording a clear demo of a song once it is finished. Enter your songs in songwriting contests—and get your work heard by record companies and recording artists.

Take the time to explore the chords, melody, and lyrics of your favorite songs, as well as ones that are unfamiliar to you. As you study a song, ask yourself what aspects made it appealing and memorable. You'll find hours of enjoyment and valuable insight listening to recordings and reading through sheet music as you analyze the best (and worst) of American popular music. If you play the guitar or piano, you should obtain a complete chord fingering chart for your instrument. You may also wish to pursue an in-depth study of chord forms and structure, as is provided in any good music theory textbook. This further study is particularly advisable for those who wish to arrange their music. A basic understanding of the more advanced theoretical aspects of written music can only serve to enhance your ability as a songwriter. However, at this point, you have all the skills you need to create successful songs in many styles.